£ 4.G₁ —

Project
Water Horse

Project Water Horse

The true story of the Monster quest at Loch Ness

Tim Dinsdale ARAeS

Routledge & Kegan Paul
London and Boston

First published in 1975
by Routledge & Kegan Paul Ltd
Broadway House, 68–74 Carter Lane,
London EC4V 5EL
and 9 Park Street,
Boston, Mass. 02108, USA
Set in 11 pt. Ehrhardt
and printed in Great Britain
by Ebenezer Baylis and Son Ltd
The Trinity Press, Worcester, and London

ISBN 0 7100 8029 8 (C)
ISBN 0 7100 8030 1 (P)

To Alex Campbell,
who started it and who has stood firm ever since

Contents

Plates

Preface

There have been several books written about the phenomenon of the Loch Ness Monster, and one about its cousin in Loch Morar. These contain a mass of verbal testimony, historical information and some evidence which is real, and even provable.

Having committed the sin of writing three of these myself, I dare not impose *The Beastie* further on the public, because it has come to be regarded by the national majority as something of a pet, and by a minority as a damned nuisance.

But as no one seems to have written about the chase – the actual monster-hunt, as it affects the individual and the populace at large, and as I have been so much involved with it, if for no other reason than to pacify my publishers I venture now to put pen back to paper – or, if I am honest, to peck at an aged typewriter, in the hope that no one will throw stones at me when they come to read the book.

T.D.

Acknowledgments

Due to the span of years, and the multitude of events covered by this book several pages would be needed to record the names of all those kind souls to whom I owe a debt of thanks. Let me therefore just say as simply as I can: 'Without your help and encouragement this story would not have been written, and we could not have progressed as far as we have at both Loch Ness and Loch Morar.'

At a more personal level, and in particular where the problem and hazard of sustained boatwork is concerned, I need to thank especially Jim Ewing; the brothers Carruth of St Benedict's; Alex Campbell; Basil and 'Freddie' Cary; Dick and Phyllis Jenkyns; Guy and Angela Prendagast. For scientific aid and comradeship I must thank Dr Eric Blank of Sheffield University; the Loch Ness Investigation Bureau; the Academy of Applied Science; the National Institute of Oceanography; the Kodak Awards team; the Loch Morar Survey; the Royal Photographic Society; the Society for Investigating the Unexplained. In terms of 'the media' I would like to thank the many friends and helpers made in radio, television and the press, who have helped to put the facts across; and in cinema, Ken Peterson of Walt Disney Productions, who animated 'Nessie' in a way no one else could do. And, where PR is concerned, the British Tourist Authority in London and New York deserve to be congratulated. Equally, Bob Rines of the Academy has my thanks and admiration for his unending enthusiasm, generosity and dynamic support.

I am indebted to the following copyright holders: Plate 7, the BTA; Plate 4, Ivor Newby; Plate 17, Nicholas Witchell; Plate 19, Academy of Applied Science and Raytheon; Plates 20, 21 and cover design for this book, Klein Associates, Inc; Plates 22 and 23, Academy of Applied Science and Loch Ness Investigation Bureau Ltd.

1
In retrospect

It was the twenty-seventh day of September 1967, and I was conscious of becoming technically a year older. At forty-two, with a family of splendid youngsters to support, my adult behaviour during the past decade left much to be desired, when judged by the standards of convention. And yet despite that I was happy. Harassed but happy, penniless but free, and treated with fond good humour by the progeny, because I had given up a career in aeronautics to embark on a form of madness of which they thoroughly approved – the pursuit of a legendary monster.

And here I was 'at it' again, perched high up on the southern shore of Loch Ness, gazing down at the inky windswept waters, stretching to right and left in gigantic panorama.

Half paralysed by the cold I stood muffled in an old Canadian parka jacket, then leaned forward to peer through the telescopic lens of a ciné camera.

The faintly luminous image I perceived was of distant water ripples, and a graceful flight of snowy gulls, perhaps as much as a thousand yards away, and yet through the miracle of photographic optics I knew a film taken of them would enlarge to life-size on a screen.

It gave me a feeling of power; at the touch of a trigger button I could master the environment, and record once more on film the incredible fact, which I had tried so hard to establish over the years – the bona fide existence of enormous unknown aquatic animals in Loch Ness.

Thinking back, my mind skipped through time to the moment in early 1959 when a rolled-up package poked through the letter box, containing a copy of *Everybody's* magazine, now long out of circulation. In it I had found an article on the Monster, in which, of course,

I did not believe; but I had found something else besides – a thread of interest, which had grown as I studied it, until it wrapped itself around me like the coils of an anaconda. There was simply no escape and after months of study, probing and collecting and analysing information, I reached the conclusion others had reached before me, that the Loch Ness Monster was not a fake or a case of mistaken identity, but a massive living entity, of flesh and blood – or rather, a group of living entities; a colony of separate animals of extraordinary appearance, and unknown species. A study of the literature which already existed on the subject also indicated that they had originated in the sea. Since the period of the last Ice Age, the crust of the earth in Northern Scotland has buckled and risen slowly. Today, Loch Ness, which was previously an arm of the sea, stands 50 ft above sea level.

Fired by the dramatic content of this analysis, in April 1960 I drove the 600 miles from my home in Berkshire to Loch Ness, armed with a borrowed 16 mm ciné camera and telephoto lens – and watched from different vantage points around the 60-mile perimeter. It is an impressive place, some 24 miles in length and 2 miles wide at one end, narrowing to about 1 mile at the other. A third of it is over 700 feet deep, going down almost sheer from the towering walls of rock on either side, which rise in places to over 2,000 feet.

Loch Ness forms a link in the chain of lakes and waterways, known as the Caledonian Ship Canal, joining the western and eastern seaboards; through it fishing vessels and yachts would pass each day – in small flotillas, keeping company through the lonely mountainous cleft.

Six rivers and innumerable burns run into it. A modern motor road runs the length of the north shore, carrying a weight of tourist traffic in summer, between the village of Fort Augustus to the west, and Inverness, ancient capital of the Highlands, to the east. Originally blasted out of the rock, the road is now largely obscured from the loch by a natural fence of scrub and saplings which has grown up since its construction in the early 1930s – the time when the 'Monster' first made international news. Probably the thunderous blasting and the fall of rock caused a disturbance which brought the Monster to the surface more frequently than usual; for that period of time produced the greatest number of sightings, with more than eighty-four recorded in the month of August 1933.

People spoke much of the same phenomenon – a huge water disturbance and V-wake, with sometimes the back of what appeared to be a large living creature on the surface. Humps and bumps were described by different people, and on rare occasions a long serpentine neck appeared with a small head at the extremity.

Sometimes the Monster basked on the surface – particularly in calm sunny weather; and sometimes it moved with great rapidity. On a few occasions too it had been reported actually out of water!

Whatever the origin of these reports, the homework I had done convinced me there was truth in some of them and this view was strengthened on questioning witnesses at first hand. Furthermore, the very size of the loch and its huge natural content of fish – migrating salmon, trout, char, pike and eels in the bottom silt – suggested there was both space and food for large predators, no matter what their species.

To most, the Monster appeared incredible, and I realized that I was in pursuit of something as technically unlikely as a unicorn; but the hard work put in on the shores of the loch with the camera, from dawn to dusk each day, produced results.

On the sixth day, at 9 a.m. I saw and filmed a member of the colony from a point high up on the southern shore. The camera was mounted inside the car, but I examined the object through binoculars first, before beginning to film. I saw it very clearly, with the sunlight shining on it, and while viewing it, the Monster (for monster it was in size) came to life and surged away across the water, slowly submerging and then turning abruptly left, close to the far shore, and proceeding underwater for half a mile, trailing a great wake behind it. I shot about forty feet of black-and-white film of the animal, then later filmed a boat steering the same course, for comparison.

In the months following, due largely to the BBC's 'Panorama' programme, and a world-wide newsfilm release through United Press, this film caused a re-awakening of interest – though officialdom remained aloof.

It was this very lack of response which was so puzzling. The Monster's existence represented a momentous find, in terms of zoology, and human interest too, but there was no sign of any nationally-sponsored programme of research, which was what was obviously needed. Loch Ness was a big place.

The alternative was for individuals to continue working privately in the hope of obtaining better evidence, close-up film of the creature on the surface – close enough to show its spots.

At a private level I had to decide what next to do about it, because after filming the Beast in 1960 it soon became apparent to me that industry would not tolerate any serious outside interest. I had a good job at the time, but had to make up my mind whether or not to resign it.

The decision was not too difficult to make, because it was clear that unless I did, I would probably get the sack; for the Monster kept getting in the way, imposing more and more on my time and mental concentration.

I left, and for two months during the summer months 'rested' at home; and during this blissful period achieved a lifelong ambition. I started to write.

It is hard work for the beginner, and to recuperate between bouts on the typewriter I would sit outside in a deckchair, and doze in the sunlight, with the colours of the garden about me, and the chatter and patter of small folk busy at play.

Of our four children, my eldest daughter, then about five, was an elfin golden child, for ever playing with her friends, who would go and come as they pleased.

Sometimes with eyes closed, feigning sleep, I would feel the light touch of her fingers – and 'awake' to a chorus of giggles to find my hair tied up with bits of string and ribbon, and pockets bulging with peculiar oddments. In time I came to be accepted, and was shown off to the more rare and timorous visitors from further up the street in much the same way a new toy or dolls-house would be – something special, a genuinely tame grown-up who could be used for games without objecting. I never interfered – and was handsomely rewarded, for in playing Gulliver, I was allowed to re-enter the world of children, which is a very secret place.

It was a time that was all too short and when I joined the 'Advanced Projects Group' of a huge aeronautical combine, I also joined the army of commuters who daily wend an interminable way to the metropolis and back.

Seconded to an office near Piccadilly, I was rattled at by typewriters and computing machines, and half choked by wreaths of smoke, and the hot air engendered by overcrowded meetings.

The Monster, too, would not be disregarded, and I found myself writing furiously to escape the insane monotony of commuter travel. Back and forth, back and forth I would go, and yet in every situation there is an element of humour. I knew I was trapped, and so, like a prisoner in his cell, took delight in seeking freedom, odd scraps of it, and this I would use to further the progress of the book. I scribbled at every opportunity and, inevitably, late into the night at home, for it was the only way to get it done.

In due time, with one of the periodic convulsions that afflict the British Aircraft Industry, the department was run down and the staff made redundant. I noted with some satisfaction that I was the first to go.

Back at home 'resting' once more, I reviewed the situation. The industry in Britain was in a poor way, thanks largely to the inept and futile dealings of post-war government, but with a young family and the Monster to contend with I was loth to go abroad.

Besides, the real issue at Loch Ness went much deeper than one might at first suppose. I was not a zoologist, and therefore had no reputation to gain or lose in establishing the facts – but I was an engineer and practical scientist, and had seen enough of life around the globe to realize that the fundamental principle of truth was worth defending.

I had now to decide whether to stand on the issue, or retire to a position of safety. My career was clearly in the balance, because I could not go on with it and at the same time tackle the Monster – but without the assurance of an income how could we live?

Inwardly, the question of ethics was already resolved, but the problem of economics was different. As a bachelor, I would simply have moved up to Loch Ness, taken a part-time local job, and embarked on a continuing watch until I succeeded in getting a better film – but whatever the situation, man is bound by practicality and for two months I spent my time answering advertisements, though none of these was for work overseas.

And then, quite unexpectedly, the problem solved itself. I went into business as a salesman; which gave me independence until 1968.

During this period I was able to put eight private expeditions into the field. Battle was joined, but I was soon to find it more of a war of attrition, because during the first four years I became engaged on a series of adventures which did not go well.

They were all sited at the same spot, and I would refer to it as 'the place marked X', because it was not shown on the inch-to-the-mile Ordnance Survey map; and needed an X to point it out.

It was situated to the east of Foyers Bay on a strip of beautiful, inaccessible shoreline. To get there involved climbing 150 ft up the steeply wooded shore, along a narrow track then down again through a tunnel of foliage, beneath the trunk of a fallen tree, steeply, to a tiny shingle beach, perhaps 20 yards in width; with an old tumble-down wooden boatshed set up against the mountainside; so overgrown it was like a cave in appearance.

Completely secluded, it made a natural hide where I could set up my cameras and equipment in ambush, and during the 480 hours I spent watching from there, when I needed food I could leave the equipment behind unguarded. And yet, despite these advantages there was something odd about 'the place marked X'.

Four of the five expeditions based there resulted in illness or injury, or accident of a most unpleasant nature, and I became aware of some strange influence which seemed to be malevolent and prompted me to examine the background history of the area, and to research the 'Water Kelpie' legend in particular.

I am not unduly superstitious, but I do subscribe to the belief that in cases where intense human desire or emotion has been involved, purely psychic influence can have a physical effect on people, and sometimes on material objects. I have witnessed such phenomena, which absolutely defy the physical laws as we understand them; and in this an element of timelessness is often characteristic, as in the case of a haunted house where a centuries-old murder has been committed, because people today – some people – may be conscious of an evil influence, and see an apparition which terrifies them.

Certainly, at 'the place marked X', despite the quiet and beauty there, I was conscious of some dark influence. Whether or not it could be attributed to the shadows cast by local history, or something else besides, remains a matter of conjecture. But it is a fact that my research uncovered much that was unexpected.

For example, within a short distance of the spot there are the remains of two ancient forts and the sites of two other battlefields, where local clansmen massacred each other. The history of Foyers, too, is steeped in the brutality of centuries gone by, when 'Butcher Cumberland's' Redcoats occupied the area.

Indeed the history of Foyers is a book in itself, and it is only possible to glance at it in relation to my own experience.

Going a very long way back, to prehistoric times, perhaps as far as 2000 BC local tribesmen built a fort overlooking the Pass of Inverfarigaig (as it is today) 2 miles to the east. The vitrified remains are built up of rings of stone molten together by the heat of huge fires. The original inhabitants of the district were neolithic Iberians, and thereafter the ferocious Pictish tribes settled in the area, creating the Pictish Kingdom with its capital at Inverness.

Another prehistoric fort was sited where the ruins of Castle Urquhart stand today, at Strone Point on the north shore, some 5 miles farther east. Through the barbarous times of medieval history the castle came under siege on no less than six occasions, and was once held by Bruce against the English King Edward III.

In contrast, in 1115 the bishopric of Moray was founded, and the parish church of Foyers and Boleskine came into being.

At about this time the Picts became dispersed, due to Scots infiltration, and the frequent Norse invasions along the Moray Firth. The Gaelic tongue eventually replaced the Pictish as the language of the North, and the Roman Catholic church displaced the Celtic church. The Scottish feudal and clan system came into being. In the thirteenth century the Grants had large estates in the Foyers and Stratherrick districts, but gradually their influence and holdings dwindled and they migrated to Glen Moriston on the north shore

B

opposite and further west. The Frasers took their place, acquiring land first by marriage through the Grants.

The Fraser clan, of Norman stock, did not settle in the area until the fifteenth century, and thereafter shaped the history of Foyers over several hundred years. The final blow to the Grants came in 1479, when Laurence Grant of Foyers and Boleskine insulted the young bride of Gruer Mor (Big Gruer) when on a visit there. Gruer, who was also the Laird of Port Clair (Fort Augustus) was so infuriated that he gathered his clan and set forth in galleys to do battle with the Grants. They met at a small bay a mile west of Foyers, and fought the battle of 'Camus Mherbh Dhaoine' – the 'Bay of Dead Men', as the place is still called today. The Grants were defeated, and Laurence slain while trying to escape.

The clan structure was strong in Scotland, and although serfdom had long been abolished, the tenants of an estate like Foyers were intensely loyal to their chief, who could call them to arms. In consequence, feuds and rebellions were commonplace. In 1603, Hugh Fraser, fifth of Foyers, became involved in a feud between two different clans. The MacDonalds of Glengarry and the clan MacKenzie. A battle resulted on the slopes of Mealfuarvonie, the great bald-headed mountain opposite Foyers on the other side of Loch Ness. The battle of 'Lan-na-Fala' the 'Meadow of Blood' was fought with the usual wild ferocity, and the MacDonalds were defeated. Their leader, Allan of Lundie, who had previously set fire to a church full of MacKenzie women and children, escaped, jumped into the loch, and was rescued by Hugh Fraser who came across in a boat.

The Frasers fought outside Scotland too, with Lord Lovat's army which invaded England in 1650 in support of King Charles II, but was disastrously defeated at Worcester.

Cromwell restored some measure of order when he invaded Scotland in return in 1655, and subdued the warring factions around Loch Ness by garrisoning troops at Inverness and Inverlochy (Fort William), and by patrolling the loch with a warship.

In the first Jacobite rising, William Fraser, eighth of Foyers, supported the government of George I, and was attacked by neighbouring clans and even septs of his own, the Frasers, and was forced to hide in the hills when his estates were burned and plundered. Later, an inter-clan bond was signed for mutual defence, but James Fraser, ninth of Foyers, was friendly with the thirteenth Lord Lovat and his clan took sides with Bonnie Prince Charlie on the blood-soaked turf at Culloden in 1746.

Prince Charles fled westwards, and hid for a time in Gorthleck farmhouse on the Foyers estate. James Fraser escaped also and spent seven years in hiding, one favourite place being a cave close to the Falls of Foyers. As an aftermath to the battle, the Duke of Cumberland's troops garrisoned at Fort Augustus brought misery and death to the local populace. At a funeral at Foyers, one of the hungry mourners stole a loaf of bread from a passing provisions cart. The soldiers retaliated by firing into the crowd. On another occasion a boy taking a cask of beer to the Laird of Foyers in his hiding place was caught, but refused to lead the soldiers to it. In reprisal they cut off his hands.

Terrible deeds like these are hard to imagine in the tiny village of Foyers today, but, crimes of violence apart, there is another aspect of local history which is peculiar, to say the least. Passing reference is made to it in the quite serious book *Exploring the Occult* by the late Douglas Hunt MA, in chapter fourteen. It concerns the infamous, eccentric Aleister Crowley, about whom much has already been written.

But, if we are to lump all the black deeds and 'hocus pocus' together we must lose the perspective bestowed by time – in this case the passage of centuries, and the balance of what is good in human beings and their more noble undertakings.

Today, 'the place marked X', and this whole section of shoreline no longer exists. It has been obliterated, buried under the engineering works of the Foyers hydroelectric scheme, in which may be found all that is best in modern technology – ingenuity, daring, imagination, potential, and colossal subterranean structures as big as a cathedral. If the scars which mark its birth today are ugly, they will tend to heal; and if its success is as great as it deserves to be the name of Foyers will once more stand in the history books – owing nothing to the past.

In October 1964 I had watched the waters from the battlements of Urquhart Castle for two weeks, with a small team of adults, members of LNPIB – the Loch Ness Phenomena Investigation Bureau Ltd, a purely voluntary organization founded in London in 1961 to investigate the evidence and put expeditions in the field. It was the tail-end of the Monster-hunting season, but we enjoyed the comradeship and the splendid autumn colours. It made a welcome change from my solitary research, so again in 1965 I ran a crew for them, made up almost entirely of Americans.

It was fun, despite the appalling weather, the worst July for over a hundred years, but it was obvious the 'Bureau' was self-sufficient – and that henceforward I should concentrate on exploring new methods and techniques.

Having no reserve of money, this was a problem, but after years of walking a financial knife-edge I came to regard this most harassing aspect of the chase with equanimity; and to accept it as inevitable. It had not all been up-hill work. Until 1964 the illustrated talks I had been giving on the subject were mostly to private societies and schools. I worked on the principle of going where I was invited, and letting the invitations take care of themselves. Sometimes there would be long gaps between talks, and at others I would be travelling all over the country with scarcely time to meet commitments. It was an interesting diversion and through it I could see that public opinion was changing. The audiences, too, were beginning to alter in character, with more and more technical people making an appearance.

In 1964 I spoke at a comprehensive school in Slough, at the request of a young science master. He later contacted a friend at Sheffield University and this resulted in a first invitation from any university, which in turn led to many others, including a tour in 1966 of the four Scottish seats of learning as guest speaker to their Biological Societies – something of a precedent, perhaps, for an aero-engineer!

Of all the subsidiary activities this proved to be the most rewarding because a steady stream of volunteers flowed from these talks towards the LNPIB, which needed them: the young zoologists and biologists of the future.

Without doubt the year 1966 was encouraging, for in that year the Monster donned a cloak of near-respectability.

In January, the Joint Air Reconnaissance Intelligence Centre (JARIC) of the RAF reported on the film I had shot six years before, and vindicated it. Previously, the LNPIB had gained the help of this highly specialized department, and results were so rewarding that David James, their executive director and a Member of Parliament suggested that I might submit my own film, which had remained on the shelf awaiting a proper analysis.

Certainly JARIC were expert – but in my view more important still, unprejudiced, and equipped with the best optical devices for studying long-range photographs. Heir to a famous wartime tradition, when they had first spotted the German Peenemunde rocket launching sites from microscopic indications on a photograph, they examined the film, and produced a reserved and technical report based on pure mensuration (measurement) of the original filmed image, which I had so carefully preserved.

They stated flatly that it was *not* a surface or submarine vessel – 'which leaves the conclusion that it probably is an animate object'.

Furthermore, the object had a cross-section through it not less than 6 ft in width and 5 ft in height; and was travelling at approximately 10 m.p.h.

Bearing in mind that I had included a local motor boat for comparison in the film (sent out two hours later, when water and light conditions were similar), the accuracy of these calculations could be checked, because I had measured the boat in length and beam.

The report indicated that at 1,600 yards, on the basis of angles and measurement, the boat was 13·3 ft in length – whereas in fact it was 14 ft exactly. A conservative error of one inch in 7,200 establishing the JARIC report for what it truly was: a brilliant piece of detective work, of real significance.

The effect this report had on the scientific community was noticeable, though predictably the hard core of dissenters remained outwardly unimpressed; and I recognized once more the vital need for film which was not subject to interpretation – close-up film of the Beast.

1........4ᵗʰ ....19.66   Copy No. 1.. of 2

<u>JOINT AIR RECONNAISSANCE INTELLIGENCE CENTRE(UK)</u>

<u>Photographic Interpretation Report No 66/1</u>

LOCH NESS

References: A.   LOCH NESS Phenomena Film Report concerning
                   1960 (DINSDALE) sighting TD/LNPIB/2 dated
                   18th November 1965.
             B.   CRE letter CRE/S388/Prog dated 5th January 1966.
             C.   MOD DI 26(Air) letter S208/E.99/MIN(RAF) dated
                   21st December 1965.
             D.   JARIB(UK) Order No A1/66.

1.   Material examined has been the original 16mm film.   NO
copies have been made.   All examination has been by optical
enlargement of the film thus obviating losses by photographic
processes.   The majority of the examination and mensuration
has been made at 20x enlargement.

2.   This report deals firstly (paras 3 to 11) with ▓▓▓
▓▓ secondly with interpretation or deduction based ▓▓▓
▓▓▓▓▓▓▓▓ ▓▓ analysis of the mensura▓▓▓▓▓▓▓

▓▓▓▓▓▓▓▓▓▓▓▓▓▓▓▓▓▓▓▓▓▓▓▓▓▓▓▓▓▓▓▓▓▓▓▓ 16 feet.
W▓▓▓▓▓▓▓▓▓▓ of p▓▓▓▓▓▓▓▓▓▓▓▓▓▓ the ma▓▓▓um speed,
regardless of p▓▓▓▓▓▓▓▓▓▓▓▓▓▓ by the waterline
length eg the 14 f▓▓▓ with Sea▓▓▓ outboard at 6½ to 7 mph is
probably at or near its maximum possible speed.   The object is
travelling at 10 mph and it is doubtful if a 'non-planing' hull
of under 16 ft could achieve this speed.   A power boat shell
with planing hull could easily achieve and exceed this speed
and the design is such that it could appear to have a continuous
surface.   However these craft are normally painted in such
a way as to be photo visible at any time and in any case the
existence of such a craft on the loch would scarcely be missed
by any observer.   <u>The assumption is therefore that it is NOT
a surface vessel.</u>

15.   <u>One can presumably rule out the idea that it is any sort
of submarine vessel for various reasons which leaves the
conclusion that it probably is an animate object.</u>

Figure 1   Joint Air Reconnaissance Intelligence Centre Report

Precisely how to get it remained a problem, but in terms of new equipment there had been recent advances in zoom-lens photography, making cameras effective at the waterline out to the visible horizon. If one could choose a place where the loch was at its narrowest, and where sightings were consistent, a close-to-shore appearance was always possible.

There was one such place – itself unusual because for years I had not been aware of its existence. It was there, but didn't appear to be. It was not marked on the quarter-inch Ordnance Survey map, and yet it should have been.

It promised all the seclusion I wanted, and an immense surface view to east and west; but could only be approached by water. I liked the idea of it, and in March 1966, after lecturing at Aberdeen University, instead of returning home I caught the train to Inverness and continued by bus to Foyers.

The next morning I arranged for a 'gillie' to take me out in his boat to reconnoitre *The Island*, because that is what it was, and will undoubtedly remain, despite its omission from the map.

The place proved to be much larger than I had visualized, shaped like an equilateral triangle with its apex pointing directly up the Foyers river; its broad base is crescent-shaped, a small arc of shingle perhaps 80 yards across, with the two horns pointing out into the water of the loch. It sits, like all alluvial islands, just above the surface, fenced in from the rear with a forest of newly-grown scrub and sapling: a wedge of soft earth and shingle fitting neatly into the mouth of the Foyers river.

I knew instinctively this was the right place, and looked round for somewhere to pitch a tent. The shingle, piled up by winter storms was strewn with silvered driftwood, but I found a clearing where the camera could be sited, commanding an unimpaired view to east and west to the dim extremities of the loch.

Moving gently round *The Island* in the boat, we sounded out the bottom using a float and weighted fishing line. It shelved gradually, then went down almost sheer into the abyss. To the east, the Foyers river flowed silently into the loch, creating a small lagoon with a peripheral reef of shingle, and to the west a deep narrow channel spiked with rotting tree trunks marked the boundary.

The far shore, over a mile distant, with the terraced motor road scarred across it, climbed almost vertically, to its summit in the mists, and behind it the great dome of Mt Mealfuarvonie towered into the sky. It was, I knew, the nesting place of a pair of golden eagles.

Returning across the pitch-black waters of the Ness, my gillie bent to his oars, crooning a gentle song in Gaelic – and for a little the centuries stood still. I huddled in the stern, alone with my thoughts, but when the keel grounded on the shingle I climbed out and helped to drag the clumsy old boat clear of the water, knowing that when I returned I would need a boat of my own, something safe, but portable.

In due course, I obtained an inflatable dinghy with a small outboard motor, and tried them out successfully. The boat, a 9-ft Avon, was virtually unsinkable. Blown up in sections, the entire contraption could be deflated and placed in a sack, and carried in one hand only.

During 1966 and 1967 I made four expeditions to *The Island*, to live in a tent and watch from the shingle beach. It was an idyllic spot, and on each of these adventures, lasting ten days to a fortnight, the small inflatable proved its value, due to its stability. The year before, in 1965, using a minute fibreglass car-top dinghy to ferry equipment to 'the place marked X', I had come close to losing my life in a squall and had no desire to repeat the experience. On the first trip to *The Island* I cannot have travelled much more than a 1,000 yards in the Avon dinghy, but during the years to follow I trailed it as a liferaft, over as many miles of loch-water. It also acquired a name which was to become well known to Monster hunters. The *Moo-scow*.

I was not always alone on *The Island*. After a first expedition there in 1966 a friend accompanied me – a man of learning, who was interested in the research. He had proved this the year before when mounting a private photographic expedition to Loch Morar, on the Western Highland seaboard, where similar phenomena had been reported historically. John Addey had written to me then, and came over to discuss his particular interest – the study he had made of

'Nessie' sightings in relation to the lunar cycle. This indicated surface activity at particular times, and as the moon appears to have quite definite effects on animals, and human beings too, I was glad to examine this new approach to the subject. We decided to employ every device we could think of to bring the Monster to the surface, and if possible towards us.

I knew that low-frequency sound attracted some aquatic creatures; and years before had also noted comments from a correspondent – who pointed out that *asafoetida* (described in the dictionary as 'a medicinal resin with an offensive smell') had a similar effect.

We divided responsibilities. I would build the low-frequency sound equipment, and John would obtain the *asafoetida*. After a long search, he persuaded suppliers of this rare substance, obtained from the root of a plant dug up in the deserts of East Pakistan, to import a small amount expressly for our use.

In the event, neither experiment proved successful. The *asafoetida* had smelled abominably, and my sound equipment, designed to produce a booming noise by the action of the waves, had fouled the *Moo-scow*'s propeller, before sinking to the bottom.

It was our first attempt to move from the passive, watching role of photographer, hoping to intercept another Monster surfacing; but the results were not encouraging, and to continue indefinitely without success was not an easy thing to do.

Over the years, there had of course been a number of 'final' expeditions, and I had once gone as far as to dispose of my expedition shoes: an old pair of brogues which I used on the first successful trip in 1960. In the time between they had worn away into holes and had carried me on countless photographic sorties. I had intended dumping them in the loch the year before as proof of finality, but somehow couldn't bring myself to do it. I left them on *The Island* instead, for it was such a splendid place. Returning in 1967, alone, I could not find them, for they had disappeared beneath tons of shingle moved in the winter storms – but I had weathered the storms too, though of a different nature.

It was a long hunt and I watched perhaps sixteen hours a day, cooking meals in the open in full view of the water. I would get up at dawn, having slept in an old camouflaged army tent in which were assembled all the boxes and equipment. There was the usual bewildering weather, with squalls, sunshine, rain and calms, booming thunderstorms and wreaths of unearthly mist in the very early morning – for Loch Ness is meteorologically unstable. Sometimes clouds at different levels could be seen moving in opposite directions up and down the loch.

A strange place, and living close to nature, in a little while, when the birds and animals came to accept my presence. A small vole-like creature would appear at breakfast time, rustling the leaves to attract attention. I would hand out porridge oats, about a teaspoonful – and for a moment he would look at me, with his little beady eye, glistening black, as much as to say 'thank you very much'. Then there were the nesting oyster-catchers, the brilliant sea magpies, with their black and white plumage and scarlet beaks. Unhappily, I crushed two eggs lying on the shingle, when putting up the tent. The hen bird was so enraged that she attacked. Screaming defiance she flew into the canvas, reminding me of a scene from the Alfred Hitchcock nightmare film *The Birds*.

But, there was nothing about *The Island* which made one ill at ease. I was never lonely, though I had but two visitors throughout the course of the week, fishermen who came over out of curiosity. I was glad to welcome them, and accept a gift of trout – delectable fish, which I fried in butter for my breakfast.

The Island was in itself a retreat, its complete naturalness a harmony. As the days slipped by, time lost its meaning, and I measured the sun in its path and counted the stars above at night in the great vault of heaven.

Thankfully, I had no *asafoetida* – having by chance discovered since the previous expedition that it was used as a specific repellant by Norwegian fishermen, centuries before! The book which alerted me to our gross error of judgment was *The Great Sea-Serpent*, published in 1892 by Dr A. C. Oudemans of The Hague, a leading zoologist of the time. In this monumental work of nearly 600 pages he presented a vast amount of evidence for unknown water monsters and on page 259 the following comments are recorded:

The well-known Mr. Heinrich Rathke in 1841 published in the *Archiv für Naturgeschichte* 7th year, Vol. 1, his dissertation 'On the Sea Serpent of the Norwegians'. I am obliged to give a translation of his paper:

'On a journey which I made through Norway I availed myself of the opportunity of making enquiries after a hitherto problematical and even doubted animal, the so called sea-serpent (Soe Orm in the language of the Norwegians) . . . it appears almost every year. It is said to have been especially observed in that part of the year, viz. in the dog days, and only then when the weather is quite still and the surface of the water smooth. When after its appearance the water is ruffled, however slightly, it immediately disappears. Great is the dread of it, so that in the dog days many fishermen, otherwise intrepid, don't go far into the sea, without taking with them *asa foetida*, which is said to drive away the animal by its smell, when thrown into the water.'

Having lived with the stuff for nearly a week, I concluded that 'the well-known Mr. Heinrich Rathke' was probably right on this point; but in place of it I had brought an unusual piece of equipment of practical value – a step ladder, on top of which I perched for several hours a day.

Notwithstanding the odd looks given me by passing fishermen, I was glad to use it because at near to water level the view to the horizon is limited; but this can be increased dramatically in terms of the simple relationship – distance to the horizon in *miles* is approximately the square root of one's height above the water in *feet*.

Thus, by increasing eye-level from about 8 ft above the loch at the camera, to 18 ft on top of the step ladder I could increase my scan from approximately 2·8 miles to 4·2 miles! I knew this to be important, because when John Addey and I had been watching the year before, a vessel had passed and had later reported the Beast astern roughly in our location – but we had missed seeing it.

The aftermath to the 1967 expedition was predictable. I was

demoralized, for I had watched the water for 130 hours, again without tangible result. After twelve successive defeats in seven years I began to feel the odds were hopeless: and costs were increasing.

Hiring equipment was a constant drain on resources, and yet I could not afford to buy these cameras, and was ineffective without them. It was a vicious circle.

Then, unexpectedly, something happened which removed this fearful stumbling block. I won a scientific award, a 'Kodak Award', with which to purchase all the photographic equipment I had dreamed of. I just could not believe it, and when the crates and boxes arrived I spent the day unpacking each one carefully; checking the contents against a list, which had twenty-two separate items on it, ranging from a zoom lens, which cost over £400, to individual filters.

To an engineer, specialized equipment has a quality of its own, and in the highly competitive field of photography a great deal of effort is put into making cameras look attractive, with the result that my monster-hunting kit had an element of visual charm about it. Finished in grey and black, it had silver parts which glittered, and the lenses reflected light through an opalescent bloom – great eyes in whose limpid depths one could observe the iris, delicate interleaves of metal, controlling the aperture.

At a press luncheon, shortly after receiving this equipment I met three other Award winners, who were asked to comment on their projects. In each case the camera was the principal tool, and when my turn came I made the point that, in treating the Loch Ness phenomena seriously, Kodak was contributing to an overall study which could, in time, help to solve the mystery, which for some reason did not appear 'respectable' to science! It was not perhaps a conventional speech; but I meant every word of it.

Later in the summer of 1967, to celebrate, my wife and family travelled up to Foyers with me, and stayed at the small hotel. The weather was a disappointment, and for the first few days we could barely see the water for rain and mist. I had promised my eldest son a night or two of camping on *The Island* and when at last the weather cleared, we boated over to set up a hide, and the old bell-tent. At dusk we bade goodnight to the others who returned to the hotel. Some 200 ft up, and half a mile away, they could just see us through binoculars.

The night passed uneventfully, but in the early morning, at about 5.30 a.m. I decided to test a new type of illuminating flare, triggered from a small device the size of a fountain pen. I had warned the Loch Ness Investigation crew on the opposite shore that a white flare from our peninsula would indicate a sighting, but their base-camp at Achnahannet was 4 miles distant and I doubted if their watchers would be out so early.

The sizzling ball of magnesium, of some 5,000 candle-power, rose to a great height, then fell back into the water with a gratifying hiss.

We ate breakfast, enjoying the welcome sunlight, and at a time much earlier than expected we noticed the family waving madly to us, standing on a spit of land to the west.

Climbing into the dinghy, we motored over, curious to find the cause of all the excitement, only to learn that the LNPIB had a boat out on the water drifting through the night, and from a point approximately 2 miles to the west had seen what appeared to be the Monster's back on the surface, not far from our peninsula.

Five minutes later, by a remarkable coincidence, our white illuminating flare arched into the sky, and the boat crew immediately drew the obvious conclusion. They sailed back to Fort Augustus, and phoned a message through to their HQ at Achnahannet. The group commander rang Foyers hotel across the loch, seeking confirmation.

My wife spoke to him, and then, with the three children, came racing down the hill. When we approached, unhurried, they decided to act out the drama and pretend they knew nothing about our splendid success. Unfortunately, we knew nothing about it either. We had seen nothing, and had difficulty in persuading the Investigation people that this was truly the case – that we were not hiding a marvellous piece of film from them.

It was a galling experience, and emphasized the disadvantage of being down too close to the water. There had been no room for the step ladder on this expedition, so once again 'Nessie' had eluded us.

After carefully weighing the facts of this experience, I decided to withdraw from *The Island* too, and that is why on 27 September 1967 I found myself back where I had started years before, high up on the south shore, with a camera and long lens set up on a tripod.

2
Catamaran

Looking down over the dark ruffled waters of Foyers Bay, I felt much like an artilleryman with an immense field of view, and power at his fingertips.

After so long at the water's edge, it was a relief to retreat once more to the heights. It gave one a better sense of perspective, and although the weather was unsuitable and cold, I stayed on to peer once more through the very long lens of my camera. I could see the gulls at a point close to *The Island*, now in the far distance and looking unimportant – just a patch of furze and brush with the sweep of river swirling past.

Then I saw them take to flight, and flap lazily across the water, a pattern of snowy dots making their way eastwards. Something had disturbed them, but minutes passed before I saw what it was. A small private yacht cleared the fringe of trees lining the south-west shoreline, and motored peacefully round the point and into Foyers Bay, a clean white little craft with two or three people aboard. They dropped anchor and came ashore in the dinghy. I 'potted' them with my lens: small faces, smiling and talking in soundless animation – a long way off still. A girl and two young men in bright jerseys and faded blue trousers, and later when they returned I watched them haul the anchor and set off down the loch.

In perhaps 1,000 hours of watching I had seen many craft in transit through the loch, mostly plodding on motor power, and occasionally some great ocean-going yacht showing her paces by tacking back and forth under sail. All kinds of craft, from the solid working hulls of trawlers to noisy powerboats kicking up the spray, and an old-fashioned steamboat converted to carry passengers.

Boats on Loch Ness were uncommon at that time. It was a transit channel. They travelled through each day, remote and purposeful.

And yet, in watching this one small boat drop anchor, the illusion of remoteness was shattered. For once, the shore made contact with the boat in transit, with people on it, live people – not the tiny little dolls one saw through binoculars, sitting motionless. For once I questioned the risks of working from the water, bred of so many tales of near disaster, and my own experience. Perhaps if one obtained a boat that was large and strong enough one could live on it, anchoring somewhere at night.

It would need to be a stable craft if used for cameras, and this would mean a catamaran. A big catamaran – a great big one, with room inside, and decked-in fore and aft.

The only big catamaran I had seen was at the Earls Court Boat Show years before, in 1962. I had examined it with the eye of a layman, but it impressed me. The view of it I could remember was from astern – the hatch door open, leading inside, the varnished woodwork set against the white of the hull, and the great wide cockpit aft. The mast seemed almost to go up through the roof. Clearly it was a yacht for millionaires; and I passed it by admiringly.

A week later, at home once more from my expedition, I played golf with a friend. I told him about the catamaran and my need to acquire one, and why. As my accountant, he was used to these idiosyncrasies, and played a number four iron shot neatly down the fairway before replying.

'Do you remember old so-and-so?' he said, 'we played a round with him a month or two ago.'

I said I did.

'Well,' he said, 'he's a yacht broker with Interyacht at Chichester I'm playing a game with him on Thursday, so I'll mention it.'

He did; and two days after that, I received a specification, a diagram and a photograph of the catamaran *Makita*; an 8-metre Bobcat moored in the Chichester yacht basin. She had twin outboard motors and all the usual gear. She was up for sale at £1,900; more than £1,000 below her original selling price.

I glanced through the specification, with interest, though much of it was jargon to me. 'Length O.A. 26′3″ – Beam 14′ – Draught 1′9″', that much I understood, but 'Bermudian Sloop – Mast in tabernacle' conjured up an impression of something foreign and faintly spiritual. 'Mast in tabernacle' – could there be candles too at the point where it fixed into the hull, and a bearded Rabbi stowed in the dunnage locker?

Looking down the list I noted 'Stainless steel standing rigging, and Terylene running rigging' and then 'Gibb roller reefing'; it all seemed very athletic. There were 'two mast winches' and 'two sheet winches'. Further down I could see that 'accommodation' allowed four adults and two children to sleep on board, in great comfort on Dunlopillo mattresses. I wondered if the 'sheet winches' were used for hauling up the bedclothes.

Intrigued, I read on. *Makita* had 'Twin Evinrude 2 cylinder, 18 horse-power petrol outboard', etc., etc. – the 'equipment' included a pulpit (again the spiritual influence), anchor, chain, warps, fenders, boathook, sail cover, cockpit cover, helmsman's seat, bathing ladder, compass, barometer, Pal D/F, echo sounder, patent log, radar reflector, navigation lights, charts.

This, in addition to all the mass of other equipment indicated to me that the boat had been designed for deep-sea sailing, but when I read the last entry in the specification, under the heading 'General Remarks' I was very much surprised.

I read something which, under the circumstances, seemed hardly credible: 'The O'Brien 8-metre cruising catamaran is probably the most popular catamaran built in the U.K. – *Makita* was the 1962 Boat Show exhibit, and has proved to be a most satisfactory cruising yacht.'

The boat which I had been thinking about – the one I had so clearly in my mind's eye – was the actual boat awaiting inspection at Chichester!

Spurred on by this most remarkable coincidence, I immediately set to work to find a sponsor, and opened a file with the title 'Project Water Horse', which was later to become the most bulky folder in my cabinet.

Having by now spoken to the yacht broker on the phone I found out that *Makita*'s owners were living in Rome, and that they were eager to sell. I was advised to make an offer as soon as possible because she was a 'good buy'.

C

Clearly the next step was to draw up a plan and cost out the operation.

1 I would obtain a sponsor.

2 Inspect the boat, and, if suitable, purchase her outright.

3 Lift her by road to a Thames-side slipway near my home in Reading.

4 Careen and repair and generally make her ship-shape.

5 Load up in early May, and then sail her down the Thames, through the Port of London and out into the Channel. From there I would sail northwards along the coastline, calling in at night at ports to anchor, all the way to Inverness, and the eastern end of the Caledonian Ship Canal – a journey of some 1,000 nautical miles.

6 I would allow one month for the journey, and possible bad weather, then spend three months (June to August inclusive) on Loch Ness before sailing out the other way, and back down the west coast of Britain: back to the Chichester mooring where she would be put up for sale once more.

7 The whole expedition would take five to six months, allowing for contingencies, and would mean giving up my business and the small income that resulted.

Working out the figures, based on a purchase price of £1,200 (assuming such an offer was accepted) and allowing £300 for refit, I reckoned operating costs would run to another £1,500 if I lived in the very simple and economical way to which I had become accustomed.

The problem of a crew on the sea journey in both directions might be solved by inviting volunteers to come aboard, and work for the fun of it, and pay their way as well. It was feasible, because I knew several amateur sailors who would jump at the opportunity. But the greatest stumbling block remained myself. I had never even sailed a canoe. I knew not the first thing about it, and this might serve to damp enthusiasm, because the North Sea could be very rough and dangerous, and amateurs like to serve under an experienced skipper.

However, it was not impossible, and having mastered the art of flying aeroplanes I did not feel that learning to sail would prove too difficult; but for one so ill-equipped financially, it was an ambitious scheme, and when I thought about it I realized there was a great deal that could go wrong.

The first approach I made was to a vast organization, the Thompson Group of newspapers, to both *The Times* and *The Sunday Times*, but on 4 December 1967 I was informed politely that neither wished to sponsor the project.

On 10 December I prepared an even longer letter and proposal – a small brochure in fact, which I sent to David James at the LNPIB, with copies to two other directors including the chairman, Mr Norman Collins, who was also a Director of ATV.

The idea put forward was basically as outlined, but when on the water at Loch Ness I would have aboard a camera and crew from their watching team, each day, and maintain a second crew ashore on *The Island*, camping out.

In this way, every member of the changing shore watch crews would filter through for camera training, and in so doing spend 24 hours on the boat and 24 hours ashore under canvas. It was an appealing idea, and one that made sense, and on 13 December I received an encouraging letter from Norman Collins in reply:

> I have always been whole-heartedly in favour of co-operated
> effort, and I know that David shares this view. I feel sure
> that the other members of the Bureau are of the same opinion.
> In other words, the principle is agreed and it is purely a matter
> of working out the plan.

On receiving this letter I made arrangements to travel down the weekend before Christmas to view *Makita*, and asked a friend to accompany me – Jim Ewing, the Scot who had helped with the inflatable dinghy, and who knew a great deal more about boats than I did. A major decision would have to be taken and I had no wish to make a bad mistake.

We travelled down through the wintry countryside of southern England. It seemed an odd time of year to be looking at boats, but on turning off the road towards the yacht basin, a forest of masts greeted us. Yachts, cruisers, dinghies and runabouts were moored there in hundreds – a new world to me entirely, because although I had travelled by ship across the face of the oceans, the only sailing boat I had ever been in was a small plywood dinghy, moving imperceptibly on a Canadian lake in northern Ontario.

I could remember at the time trying to stifle a yawn. The owner was an enthusiast, and I had no wish to offend him. Powerboating I could understand, with all the spray and excitement, but creeping about under the influence of little or no wind at all was not my idea of enjoyment.

We approached the offices of Interyacht, a part of the central building, and within minutes were shown the way down towards the water. Long wooden jetties projected out like fingers, and I noted the astonishing beauty of design in some of the larger yachts: the highly-polished woodwork and towering alloy masts festooned with a filigree of rigging – breathtaking beauty.

Approaching the end of the jetty we found *Makita*, the 8-metre Bobcat, demurely tied up awaiting our inspection. She had a tall mast too, but her shape was fundamentally different. From the beam she appeared smaller than I had expected, and the cabin amidships was obscured by an old and tattered tarpaulin draped over the boom. Stepping aboard gingerly from astern we clambered over the cockpit rail – to gain immediately an impression of width, and stability. The main hatchway door unlocked to show us the interior: a roomy cabin, with galley to starboard, a folding table amidships and flushing toilet to port. There were cupboards and drawers in profusion, and forward of the bulkhead was the main sleeping quarter, with two single berths and a double. Windows all round gave first-rate visibility from inside, and an atmosphere of spaciousness. It was impressive. I looked at Jim Ewing, who nodded. Not a word was spoken. *Makita* was obviously suitable, though once aboard I could see she would take a bit of sailing. She was not a toy boat, and had more than 3,000 sea miles recorded on the log already.

We went ashore and talked the matter over. I would offer £1,200 pending confirmation of support, and subject to an independent survey of the hull. I asked about changing the name from *Makita* to *Water Horse*, as this had been in my mind for some time, but found that *Makita* was on Lloyd's Register, and that it would cost £50 and take several months to get it altered. Apparently a new name would have to be advertised first in several journals, a requirement of law – which came as a surprise to me. I did find, however, that *Water Horse* had no Lloyd's precedent.

We departed, well pleased with the day's work, though for the first time I began to understand what I would be taking on. Loch Ness seemed farther away than it did before, and the task of sailing there more formidable. I experienced that curious tightening of the throat muscles indicated by cartoonists when they use the word 'gulp'.

During the next few days I checked on the limit permitted for wide loads on Her Majesty's Highways, and found *Makita*'s 14 ft exceeded it – though apparently by travelling at night with a special police escort she could still be moved.

There was hope for *Makita* but I was anxious about her being disposed of before I could arrange finance. When the phone rang one afternoon I answered it to find an embarrassed yacht broker on the other end, who explained she had been sold outright to an oil company executive who had looked her over the weekend before.

I was shattered, but there was nothing I could do about it. I realized too that although the 8-metre Bobcat was no longer a rarity, it was unlikely that another would come up for sale at such a price.

For three days I tried to forget my disappointment, and then with equal suddenness the yacht broker rang again. By some strange chance of fate the new owner had been posted overseas and, knowing of my interest, had instructed Interyacht to give me first refusal. Elated by this extraordinary turn of events I now felt *Makita* was only a short way from my ownership, but on 4 January when I went up to London to see the LNPIB directors the meeting did not go as expected.

During lunch we talked about the purchase, but it was soon clear that the Bureau's financial position was not yet strong enough. They were unable to help. It was another disappointment, but one I had to face. In consequence, I reverted to the only possible alternative, to approaching newspapers, and individuals of standing. It was a

forlorn and hopeless task. No one could really be expected to subscribe £3,000 to such an adventure, because with no sailing
experience, or money of my own, and debarred from commercialism
by principle, I could only appeal to the sporting instincts of people,
the majority of whom had never heard of my research, and did not
believe in the Monster.

Early in the new year I again visited the Boat Show at Earls
Court, and talked to Tom Lack, the sales director on the Bobcat
stand. I found he knew about *Makita* and was in favour of the
venture – he was a real enthusiast.

Leaving the show, I stepped outside into the rain and darkness,
taken up with my thoughts, and there, illuminated by floodlight,
Sir Francis Chichester's beautiful circumnavigating craft *Gipsy
Moth* stood proudly upright. Her tall masts reached far up into the
night. There was something splendid about her, and as I looked up
I could fancy the Southern Cross blazing in the starry sky, with the
mast-head wheeling and dipping against it. I joined the queue to
wait my turn, and moving slowly past at deck level I placed a hand
for a moment against a damaged part of the hull, where the bare
wood was exposed. *Gipsy Moth* seemed to irradiate an aura: the
intangible essence of adventure perhaps, and when I did this I knew
somehow that I would get a boat, no matter what the difficulty. It
was a strange, almost a psychic, experience.

Later I wrote to Tom Lack and explained that it was now unlikely I could raise the funds to buy *Makita* and was considering a
charter instead; if that was possible. I asked his advice, and he
replied suggesting I contact a business colleague and co-director.
He owned an almost new Bobcat moored in Loch Ryan, off
Wigtown on the Scottish west coast, no more than 200 miles by sea
from Fort William, and the Caledonian Ship Canal.

On 1 February I wrote directly to him, putting my case briefly,
and suggesting a charter covering a period of two months:
September and October.

He replied politely suggesting as an alternative that I contact a
Mr I. W. F. Smith, who lived near Glasgow; owner of 'Cat. No. 82'.

With the last applications pending for help over *Makita*, I could
afford to wait just a little longer; but one by one they failed, and on

18 February I was obliged to surrender my option on her. It was a wretched thing to have to do.

'Project Water Horse' was, I now felt sure, in a very poor way; for six months it had been hanging by the thread of my own enthusiasm, and precious little else, and unless something happened quickly it was doomed.

In a final attempt at rescue, I wrote to Mr I. W. F. Smith near Glasgow on 7 March, though with little confidence. It was a short, one-page letter, very much to the point. So many words had already gone into letters without effect. If it failed (and I was absolutely certain that it would) then I would know every avenue had been explored, but on 11 March Mr Smith replied as follows:

Dear Mr. Dinsdale,

Thank you for your letter regarding the possible charter of my Bobcat in September.

I have had my boat some three years and have not yet let her out on charter, as we are all keen sailors and enjoy sailing at the weekends and summer holidays.

However, I have had a brief look at your two books and well remember seeing your film of the Beast on T.V. and I quite realize the fascination of this quest. Therefore I should be very pleased to make my boat available. . . .

It is likely that I will be in London on business later this month and perhaps you could let me know if you would like me to contact you. A few minutes chat is worth a lot of letter writing!

Incidentally, about 18 months ago we took a B.B.C. T.V. Film Unit out for an afternoon's filming on Loch Fyne to get action shots for the 'Para Handy' series. The camera man was impressed with the stability of the Bobcat for this kind of work.

Hoping this is of some interest to you.

Yours sincerely,
I. W. F. Smith

3
The Clyde

As suggested, Mr Ian Smith and I made contact during one of his journeys south on business. He was an engineer too, with past naval experience in cruisers during the Second World War. He and his family enjoyed sailing, and hoped to make a trip up to the Western Isles that summer, and could make *Cizara* available in September, delivering her to Fort William.

We discussed the charter and a figure which would put the craft within the reach of my own pocket without the need to raise funds. We both agreed, however, that a training cruise was first essential in the Clyde, so that I could finally decide the matter. I liked Mr Smith. We understood each other, and the problems that might confront us. The venture had to be of practical value and it would be pointless to charter the craft if I couldn't handle her alone.

On 14 June I caught the Royal Scot from Euston Station in London. Several hours late, after a double engine failure, the train limped into Glasgow. Ian Smith met me, and seemed not a bit put out, which was patient of him.

We set off in his car to call in at a modern bungalow and collect the remainder of the crew; Mrs Hazel Smith and their two children Roy and Pamela.

We loaded up, then drove out to Gare Loch, a narrow sea loch extending northwards from the Firth of Clyde.

The tide was out, exposing an expanse of mussel beach, with yachts and boats riding at their moorings. It was not difficult to pick out *Cizara*. She looked trim in a coat of white paint, the twin hulls distinctive. We parked the car and began to unload, passing the bundles down to the beach where clouds of ferocious midges enveloped us. There was no escape and we were soon dancing a jig for them, slapping and waving arms about in a frantic attempt to

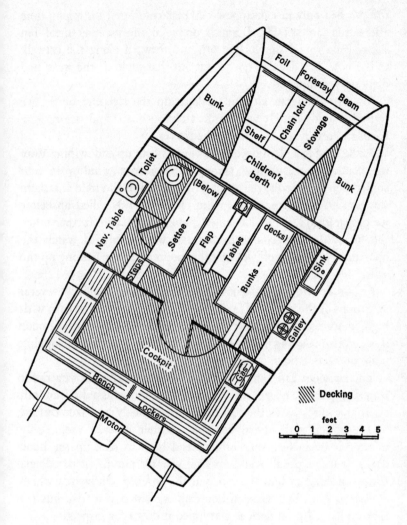

Figure 2   8-metre catamaran: layout for Mk. 1 Bobcat, Cizara

get rid of the fiery little demons. It was a relief to get into the dinghy and row out on the tranquil water where, for some reason, they ceased to follow.

Transferring the equipment, I boarded *Cizara* and found her to be immaculate. It was after 10 p.m. but due to the northerly latitude the sun had only just disappeared. Dusk continued for a long time afterwards, and as Hazel Smith prepared the evening meal Ian showed me round the cockpit aft, and forward along the catwalk to the bow. We decided not to put out that night as the wind had died away completely.

After re-arranging kit, and making up the sleeping berths we retired at midnight. It was comfortable on board and before long *Cizara*'s crew made no sound whatsoever.

Awakening to a plaintive chorus of gulls I sat up and, wiping away the condensation, glanced through the nearest window to find sunlight glinting across the water. It was tranquil and mild and there was no sign of a breeze. At 10 a.m., when all was tidied up below we prepared to leave under motor, hoping for a wind further down the loch. My first course in training was simply to watch the operations in casting off, starting the motor and later hauling up the sails.

Engine starting was electrical and, I noted, required several actuations of the button. The outboard, a 30 horse-power twin with high compression was evidently not an immediate starter, but once it was going, running in neutral it produced the muted pop-popping noise characteristic of its type.

The moment Ian Smith engaged 'forward drive' however, for some inexplicable reason it stuck in reverse and whisked *Cizara* off, stern first, directly for the rocks. Reacting quickly he seized control of the wheel, and guided her past another moored yacht, only missing it by inches, then around and back to pick up the buoy again. It was a peculiar and exciting way to start the proceedings, but we needed to find the cause of the trouble. Outboards which choose to work in reverse are curiosities, and it was with interest that we hauled it on deck and stripped it down for inspection.

Inside the motor casing a control rod end had come adrift from its shaft, and with some relief we put them back together. Mechanical failures can be tiresome at sea. The repair took an hour or so to complete, and with the motor safely back on the transom we cast off once more and headed out towards the Clyde.

A mile or so down Gare Loch *Cizara* hove to; the outboard was stopped and tilted clear of the water. Lesson number three was about to commence – the sails were going up – and with a light breeze ruffling the water I stood back in anticipation. It proved more complicated than expected. First the mainsail went up, and then the jib or staysail, extracted from a nylon bag and whisked up to the masthead. Both sails were allowed to flap free in the wind, and then, hand over hand, the mainsail was drawn in and took the wind. The smaller staysail filled, and with a great flapping and banging about the sheets, or soft Terylene ropes controlling it were pulled taut using the 'sheet winch'.

Cizara now looked more impressive, and her big mainsail carried the initials BOB in large black capitals; after Bill O'Brien, her designer, and doubling for 'Bobcat' too. Beneath, the figures eight over eighty-two, like a fraction, indicated her length in metres, and boatnumber off the slip.

At the masthead a small orange windsock pointed wind direction. By good fortune I had watched an elementary TV sailing lesson a few days previously. It was for children, but the one thing I remembered was that yachtsmen could not expect to sail closer than forty-five degrees to the wind in an average craft, and with the windsock or 'burgee' to go by one could judge this very nicely.

Cizara picked up speed and cruised down-loch with the shoreline slipping by. The breeze freshened, and seven knots was showing on the log. It was all so very silent; and as I looked astern I could see two long curling vortices of bubbles beneath the water, coming from the rudder plates on either side. It gave one an impression of speed, and curiously, of power – I had never thought of sailing boats in terms of power, and yet when I looked aloft I could see the rigging taut under the force generated by the mainsail. The impression was dynamic, and for the first time I could understand why men, and women too, were gripped by the joy of sailing. It is a powerful art, the very essence of which lies in graceful, silent movement through the water.

Sailing close to shore with the wind abeam we passed a naval shipyard, with a row of submarines moored inside the dock; black stealthy shapes hiding a complex of machinery. Beyond, the rusting hulk of an aircraft carrier lay, in process of destruction – old HMS *Leviathan*.

It was chilly on deck, and I was glad to accept a cup of steaming coffee passed up from below. I was given a turn at the wheel on the port side of the cockpit, within reach of the headsail winches. Gripping it self-consciously I held *Cizara* to her course, glancing up at the windsock – and then back to the fascinating shoreline.

By now the weather was improving. The wind dropped a little and the sun came out, summer sunshine – and to port the seaside town of Helensburgh came into view. We had travelled 6 or 7 miles already. A long stone jetty extended out towards us with naval vessels tied up to it. Noise was coming from the beach and the place was alive with bathers. I remembered it was Saturday.

We dropped anchor, and a shore party set off in the dinghy. By now the sky was cloudless and the sun blazing down. I stripped off and lay on the cabin roof, sprawled out on the dimpled fibreglass, watching the dinghy as it rowed off through the swell.

The Smiths were a delightful family – Scots to the core and to my Englishman's ear, tuned to the broad *a*s and *r*s of the south their speech was altogether different, both in accent and in the manner of speaking. To me it seemed that ordinary discussion took the form of a series of questions – queries by intonation, whereas in fact this was obviously not intended. It was a faintly musical form of speech, and before long I found myself instinctively copying it – the cadence and tone of it was refreshing to the ear.

With the dinghy back on board, hoisted on to the foredeck where it made a comfortable sunbathing couch we hauled up the anchor once more and sailed out into the deep blue waters of the Firth of Clyde. It looked more like a Mediterranean seascape than the Clyde I could remember.

During the War, in the winter of 1944, I had completed initial flying training in Britain and was awaiting a draft to Africa to continue with a pilot's course. I was detached temporarily to Yorkshire, to RAF Leconfield where three squadrons operated. They were four-engined Halifax bombers, and it was at the time of the greatest massed bomber offensive in history, which shattered Nazi Germany.

One of these Halifax squadrons was tour-expired, which meant the crews could rest and fly daylight training sorties only. These involved six- or seven-hour flights round Britain and out over the sea, and aircrew like myself who were still unqualified were allowed to fly with them to gain experience.

On one of these aerial voyages up the east coast of Scotland we flew out around the Orkney Isles, and the Outer Hebrides, and so back down the western coastline in all its craggy splendour. I spent my time in the tail gun turret, or lying in the bomb-aimer's position, with a marvellous view of the world some 20,000 ft beneath. On the return journey we had crossed the Firth of Clyde, steely grey in the wintry mists and packed with shipping. There seemed to be almost more ships than water, and I counted the aircraft carriers in particular. There were no less than thirteen of them. The whole scene stood out in relief.

A few months later I was to see the Clyde again, and board a troopship there. At ground level it was cold and miserable as we shuffled aboard, loaded down with kit. Deep into the bowels of the ship the column inched forward like a caterpillar, and at a place where there was scarcely room enough to stand the order had come back 'to make yourselves at home'. It was our mess deck, the space in which we would exist for a month, and through the stifling heat of the tropics. It was trooping at its wartime worst, and the introduction to it – the Clyde, dank and dour as I saw it then, was something I wanted to forget.

And now it seemed I had the opportunity! As *Cizara* spread her great wings to catch the breath of a following wind and floated westwards, I turned to watch the host of other craft: the yachts and dinghies all racing about or ballooning along behind multicoloured spinnakers. With four or five hours of sailing ahead I stretched out to enjoy the entertainment.

Cizara rode over the water in a silent, continuous swooping motion, dipping with the swell. To the north I could see the entrance to Loch Long, and to the west of it another loch in the dim and hazy distance – Holy Loch, the American nuclear submarine base, and a favourite place for dissidents.

Perhaps 15 or 20 minutes later a sleek black submarine went by on the surface, engines drumming through the water. She vented a mist of spray, passing within barely 100 yards of us. It was this small margin which made me appreciate the hazard posed by the multitude

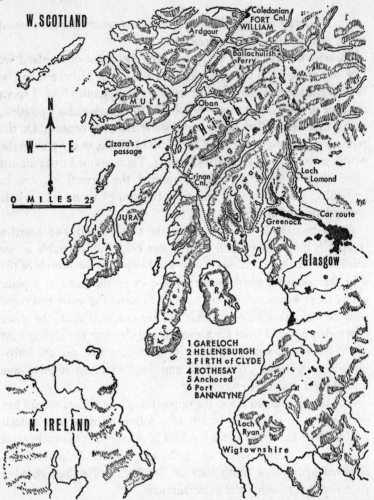

W. SCOTLAND

N
W E
S

0   M I L E S   25

Caledonian Cnl.
FORT WILLIAM
Ardgour
Ballachulish Ferry
M U L L
Oban
Cizara's passage
H i g h l a n d s
Crinan Cnl.
Loch Lomond
J U R A
Car route
Greenock
I S L A Y
Glasgow
A R R A N
K i n t y r e

1 GARELOCH
2 HELENSBURGH
3 FIRTH of CLYDE
4 ROTHESAY
5 Anchored
6 Port
  BANNATYNE

N. IRELAND

Loch Ryan
Wigtownshire

Figure 3   Cizara's *west coast passage, followed by* Malaran *in 1974*

of smaller craft. Ships' captains could do little more than hope
they wouldn't run into them. Later we saw a near collision between
an old keelboat with a varnished hull and yellowing sails, and a big
tanker coming up astern. Shouts echoed down from the bridge as
the yacht frantically put about to avoid the towering castle of metal,
astern of which the water frothed and boiled in the wake of the
great propellers.

By now we were opposite Gourock. The broad expanse of the Firth opened out ahead, and we set course to clear for Toward Point Light heading for the Isle of Bute. At two or three knots there was time to look at the scenery. The whole area was precipitous and colourful, and the activity continued. Two blunt, powerful American Navy vessels churned by, flying the Stars and Stripes, and a Royal Naval auxiliary made for the open sea, cleaving the water in a trail of fan-tail ripples. People waved, and peered at each other through binoculars. The hours passed.

Approaching the seaside town of Rothesay on the Isle of Bute, we dropped anchor to go ashore in the dinghy. It was a pleasant little place with an enclosing harbour wall packed with fishing craft. Splitting up, we wandered round the old town buildings and the crumbling remains of a castle, before returning to the waterfront. Time was slipping by, and the weather deteriorating. A cold wind was blowing from the water.

Refloating the dinghy we returned aboard to eat a hasty evening meal. The sea was uncomfortable now, so we decided to run for shelter. Hoisting sail, *Cizara* beat to windward, then turned north for the Kyles of Bute, a narrow channel close by the peninsula of Cowal. It was growing ominously dark and squalls were threatening. I watched them racing across the water, black ruffles of shadow, and when they struck, the catamaran shuddered and leapt forward across the sea, the wind whistling in her rigging. The whole craft became a living thing.

By now the light had almost gone and a mile or two to port I could barely see the wink of a buoy marking some danger spot. I could see too that in any sort of a blow the 'minimum crew of three' recommended for the Bobcat was a necessity. It would be very hard for a beginner to sail alone in a wind like that and manage all the ropes.

The first shadows of doubt crept into my mind. Was I being practical? With the deck leaping about, how could I hope to use a camera on Loch Ness, and sail the boat as well? I was tired and cold. It was past 11 p.m. and so dark one could barely see the shoreline, but *Cizara* raced on through the night, marking her passage in a trail of tumbled water. We huddled down to it, the hiss of spray and the surging powerful movement, and then quite suddenly, the wind abated. We came under the lee of the shore which rose steeply. Ahead I could just make out the shadowy hulls of yachts riding at anchor, at peace with the elements. It was a relief to find them, and with a splash of our own anchor and the rattle from its chain, for the second time in just twenty-four hours *Cizara*'s crew went below to their bunks, at midnight.

Sunday, 16 June 1968 dawned in breathless perfection: soft mists drifting over the looking-glass sea carried with them an air of unreality. The Kyles of Bute reflected the pale blue sky, and the pastel shades of green and russet brown of the Scottish mountains.

As the mists dissolved, exposing the land and sea in all its loveliness, so too the doubts and fears of the night before shrank into perspective.

If I could not sail *Cizara* alone in a storm on Loch Ness then I would have to rely on motor power, if I got caught out by one. The advantage of the craft in moderately calm water was so obvious I would be a fool not to make use of it. Having made up my mind on this point I felt better, and went below to enjoy some bacon and eggs.

We set sail after breakfast, in company with other yachts slowly cruising back towards the Firth of Clyde. The wind was scarcely noticeable, and we made perhaps two knots on the log. As the shoreline inched by we passed a large keelboat lying flat on her side on a mudflat, the tide having receded. I made a mental note of this, but realized it could not happen to a catamaran which did not have keels – only the two metal plate rudders, which hinged upwards. The cat. would take the bottom upright, and could be sailed into shallows deliberately to rest on the sand when the tide went out. I had seen photographs of this and it had struck me at the time what a great advantage it must be when cruising round the coast. One could go ashore, boat and all, without doing any damage, or getting one's feet wet!

By now progress was so lethargic that we started the motor and headed towards Port Bannatyne, a small fishing village to the north of Rothesay. We spied it through binoculars, and could see the masts and rigging of other craft. *Cizara* nosed in gently to take up a position perhaps 80 to 100 yards out, and a party went ashore to pick up milk and the morning papers.

With the crew back on board we motored slowly into deeper water, past fishing boats occupied by men and boys from the village, and as *Cizara* moved past a small lighthouse at Toward Point, the Smith children threw out fishing lines and trolled patiently for mackerel. Before long they hooked one and pulled it on deck: a small torpedo-shaped fish, barred with silver and pale translucent emerald.

For a long time now we lay becalmed off a small rocky promontory. We ate lunch there, and when staring at the featureless glassy surface I gained the curious impression that the water was turning solid, that its fluidity had diminished to the point where one might even walk on it. The illusion was spoiled by the wake from a long grey tanker, with a forest of derricks sticking up.

She moved in ponderously, and let go her starboard anchor. It plunged into the sea with a splash, and a roar from the chain, which emitted a cloud of rust as it leapt and clattered through the hawsehole. The sound echoed across the water and off the hills like a distant roll of thunder.

By early afternoon there was still no sign of a breeze, so the long journey home was started under motor. In all directions there were yachts heading back, gradually converging like motor vehicles returning to the city after a long weekend in the country.

Leaving the Clyde we steered north to the entrance of Gare Loch, and an hour later *Cizara* stopped in the water. We hitched up the mooring buoy and as her skipper made up his log we spread the big tent tarpaulin over the cockpit, sealing it in from the weather.

An hour later I was back on the motorway, and the day after that at my home in Berkshire, where nothing had changed. The brilliant sunlit panorama of sky and hills and water had disappeared as suddenly as if I had turned off a switch, but the impressions created I would never forget – and more important still, the experience had proved invaluable.

I now knew that *Cizara* could play a useful part in Project Water Horse.

D

4
Odd items of equipment

With the problem of the charter safely behind me, in July and August 1968 I started to prepare the expedition. As I gave up my business at the end of July, during the latter month I was free to work on it full time.

Practically the whole four weeks was spent in a private workshop, the big garage we had built the year before, and in due course there emerged from it an extraordinary piece of equipment which I christened the 'Cyclops Rig'. It incorporated a bit of everything: the Kodak Award cameras, a long-range sound collector, and other devices.

The Cyclops Rig represented perhaps the most unusual development in a long line of developments going back to my childhood, when I first came in contact with the 'photographic process' – the peculiar adhesive qualities of which are known to many throughout the world today.

At the age of ten I had been presented with a Brownie box camera and began to take pictures of people and places, and especially warships, because we were living in the Far East at the time and travelling by steamship from one port to another. This resulted in a succession of meetings with warships, of British, American, French and Japanese nationality in particular – all of which looked impressive and ferocious, and appeared as names or diagrams in *Jane's Fighting Ships*. To this day the sight of a warship arouses in me an almost irrepressible urge to take a photograph.

At about this time my father presented my mother with a $2\frac{1}{4} \times 3\frac{1}{4}$ Zeiss Ikon – a bellows camera of advanced design for the year 1934, which completely demoralized her. For years she had wanted a small ciné camera, because a friend had one and used it to photograph her children; but for some reason my father was against it and tried unsuccessfully to win her over to the branch of the art he understood: laborious still photography paced out with solemn exactitude. He took some very good photos too, but my mother would have none of the 'knobs and levers' on her new Ikon ... and packed it away for good.

Years later, in 1941, when working as an aero-engineering student at De Havilland, in Hertfordshire, the camera was given to me, and in taking it to bits to clean it I found the real cause of the trouble. The lens, a peerless disc of crystal, had a seven-start thread attaching it to the camera body, and at some point this had been incorrectly re-assembled. The camera was very slightly out of focus, and when I put it right I took some excellent pictures; and with the passage of years it became the first and most cherished item of photographic gear in my monster-hunting kit.

Since then there had been many additions and improvements in equipment, up to the time of the Cyclops Rig, each of which taught me something more about photography and my own ignorance concerning it. In truth there was no end to the 'photographic process' – always a beginning, but no end to it, and absolutely no escape from it.

In time, inevitably, I was to become involved in making films and experiments of one kind or another which showed that even amateurs can make a contribution.

Basically, the Cyclops Rig was designed to record a surfacing clearly, on a one-man operating principle. It had to be light, and strong, and manoeuvrable enough for one man to perform all functions of sighting, framing, light-metering, focusing, zooming, panning and speed control, without fuss – and at the same time it had to record both the operator's voice and long-range directional sound, without the two interfering with each other, or being blotted out by noise from the ciné camera.

I had first started in 1962 to use sound equipment, the object of which was to tape a quiet commentary of any sighting that occurred, while I was filming it. Accounts of the Monster had shown that it reacted to sound when on the surface, and would dive if people shouted, or slammed a car door. In the event of a close encounter, which was always possible near the shoreline I did not want to frighten it by talking out loud, but the value of a commentary describing colour, features and behaviour was obvious. It would back up the film, and in the unlikely event that the animal made a noise itself I had used a second machine, with a wide-angle sensitive microphone. Sound carries over water, reflecting off the surface, and I knew of two accounts of the Monster making 'breathing' sounds; but they had come from men in boats at night.

On the BBC's 'Your Witness' programme, on 20 July 1968, when the Monster was 'tried' before a jury of law students on TV, Alex Campbell the retired water bailiff from Loch Ness described such an experience. He had been out after dark in a small rowing boat, with the local police constable looking for poachers, when they both heard loud stertorous breathing. They did not see the beast, but he told me afterwards it was a real and unnerving experience.

What he described – or rather the sound he copied by breathing in and out loudly, making a low hissing noise through his teeth, was almost identical to the sounds made by a giant sea turtle. Great sighs, taken in as though on a deep-breathing exercise.

In view of this evidence, I decided to adapt a two-foot parabolic sound reflector to the Cyclops Rig. The reflector worked on the reverse principle of a searchlight; instead of reflecting light outwards in a parallel beam from a central point, it collected sound waves and reflected them back to focus at a central point, where a microphone was situated. But, to work efficiently it had to be sighted like a rifle, and the reflector dish had to be shielded from any unwanted noise (like the whine from the ciné camera motor). It was also a heavy object, and due to its large surface area, acted like a weather-cock in a wind.

To reduce height I mounted the dish to the side of the Cyclops Rig and counterbalanced its weight with other cameras. Using the Beaulieu camera zoom lens as a sighting telescope (it conveniently had crossed hairlines in the middle) I then set up all the cameras and zeroed them in on a target in the distance, before sighting the dish reflector.

Finally, I fitted a small mouthpiece behind the camera, an old earphone cup from a flying helmet, and attached it to a length of plastic tube. This was fed to the microphone through the sighting orifice in the dish reflector – so that when a *sotto voce* commentary was made the words would be carried directly.

With the introduction of sound in 1962 I also began to think seriously about other methods of obtaining material proof, and, returning from London one day in the train, I sketched out a small dartlike projectile with a tubular probe at the front, which might be fired from a gun or a cross-bow, with a line attached. If it struck the hide of the Monster it would punch out a core of tissue, and if barbs were attached, it might be recovered.

Curiously enough, within days I had a visitor from the LNPIB, an expedition group-commander, who had been thinking along similar lines, and we discussed the possibilities. He was something of an archer, and we both decided to do some tests independently, using a sporting long-bow. Some years later I met him again at an LNPIB function in London and inquired how it had gone, and learned that his device had 'smashed' and that he had abandoned it.

My own development nearly ended in the same way too, but over the next four years I kept improving it and ultimately perfected a projector and coring head of basic simplicity. It had followed the lines of all engineering developments, where designs are tested, then improved and retested until the faults are eliminated.

At the start I had to learn something about bows and arrows, and this meant joining the local archery club. During the next two seasons I loosed off a great many arrows with alarming inaccuracy – and was often shamed by grey-haired ladies who would stand next to me and calmly whistle arrows into the bull's-eye at a range of eighty yards. It was an intriguing sport, but I could not allow it to get a hold. I merely wanted to learn the principle and use the range to test my own bizarre equipment when no one was about.

But the first tests with it resulted in failure. The coring-head I had designed was so heavy it left the bow and flopped to the ground within yards. I had overlooked the basic principle of archery where missiles are of minimal weight, and travel at very high velocity. The system depends on kinetic energy, and in consequence I had to redesign.

The Mark II coring head weighed only a fifth as much and the first test with it was encouraging. I could not wait to use it on the archery range, which was not often available, so I hung an old carpet up in the garden and used it as a target. The arrow with the head attached pierced it, but stuck there awaiting recovery. On the second shot, it went clean through and glanced upwards in flight, falling on the roof of a neighbouring house. I went round to the owner, and sheepishly asked: 'Please can I have my arrow back?' On the next shot I attached a nylon line to prevent this happening again. I taped a small axial-spool fishing reel to the bow, with the line wound on to it, and let fly once more. The reel jammed with the arrow in flight, jerking it to the ground and damaging the head. I cursed myself for not using a dummy, but it was too late and I nearly gave up the venture. It needed hours of work to repair the coring head, and I decided to use the archery field in future, and obtain a much bigger reel and stronger line before making further tests.

Approaching the archery field one summer afternoon, I found two men harvesting the long grass with scythes. They looked up with curiosity as I put my gear together – and with astonishment when I loosed off the first shot. The bow twanged, the special arrow flew, drawing a long helix of nylon from the reel, translucent in the sunlight and giving the strange impression of a tracer shot, leaving the faintest coil of smoke – but the line jammed on the reel again.

The arrow continued in flight, stretching the nylon behind it, then started back towards me. I was in danger of shooting myself, and ducked instinctively, ending up in a snarl of shimmering nylon with the arrow sticking in the turf. But I had seen enough to prove the system. It worked, providing I could overcome the jamming.

In time I did, and during the course of the next two years the bow went with me to the loch, but my accuracy was bad and the range no more than 30 yards; barely enough to score a hit even if the Monster was patrolling close to shore. Attempts to increase the power of the bow with rubber strands were useless. It was my own strength that was lacking. I could not pull more than a certain number of pounds on the bowstring.

In 1965 I heard of a new type of cross-bow and on the journey north that year made a diversion to purchase it. It was a handsome thing, with a telescopic sight and a range of 500 yards! I tested it at my brother's farm in Northumberland and the bolt flashed out of sight. At the loch again, I let fly with a standard bolt weighing perhaps an ounce – and saw the water kick up in a plume of spray like that from a rifle bullet. It was a powerful device, which I soon learned to treat with caution, but it had potential. I spent some time developing a special arrow for it, painting it in black and yellow fluorescent stripes, then attached a small 8 mm ciné camera to the stock of the bow, to film the shot. The arrow shaft might thus act as a scaling marker, when sticking in the Monster's tough and warty hide, but it was not until 1966 that the coring head reached a final stage in development – a Mark III design.

In that year I spoke at Cambridge University at the invitation of a research scientist at the School of Veterinary Medicine, who was an expert on hypo-darting. We talked afterwards, and on the strength of what he knew about large thick-skinned animals he advised me to redesign the coring head. If I wanted to be certain of living tissue cells it would need a 6-inch probe. With perhaps 2 inches of epidermis and an inch or so of stringlike connective tissue below that to penetrate, the short probe I used was inadequate. He also pointed out that retrieval would require an effective barb arrangement.

I was grateful for this information, and returned home. Before long the Mark III coring head was in being, but I had yet to tackle the problem of the barbs. What was needed was an internal skewer, which would impale itself on the tissue sample, but again there was no easy solution. The internal diameter of the probe was only a quarter of an inch.

After some thought I made a skewer out of silver-steel and filed tiny flats on it. Snipping the tips off sewing needles, and using tweezers to forge a bend in them against a tiny forging block heated by the flame of a gas-cooker, I quenched them out in water to retain the temper of the steel. It was a smith's job in microminiature, but it was successful. All that remained to be done now was to stick the barbs on to the skewer flats with epoxy resin, and bake them in the oven.

Early on in the venture I realized that even if I got a core of tissue it would not be of much value unless I could preserve it, and find someone to analyse it. Proof of the shot, and the hit resulting, I would have on ciné film, but proof of the specimen would have to rest with someone else.

Fortunately, in the spring of 1964 I gave a talk at the Essex Institute of Agriculture, at the invitation of Dr F. Kenchington, a senior lecturer. It was an amusing interlude because the students were building a giant and fearsome model monster, which they intended to float on Loch Ness in the interests of charity. Everyone was hospitable; I was advised on preservatives by Dr Kenchington and his son Richard, and given phials of pure and formalized alcohol, and detailed instructions on how to use them.

In 1965, however, I spoke to the Zoological Society at Sheffield University, and by chance met another senior lecturer with a research interest in genetics. He kindly put me up overnight, and we discussed the tissue-sampling device, in which he showed an interest. To my surprise he told me that if I could obtain a scrap of living tissue it could be kept alive for two days by placing it in a sealed tube of nutrient media – and thereafter preserved *alive* for future study in a laboratory.

I was excited by this, and we made arrangements for fresh supplies of this special fluid to accompany me on each new expedition. I also found out what to do if by chance I was successful. Obviously, delivery of a specimen could not be delayed, and we examined the various means of reaching each other quickly, and how best to get it to a laboratory.

What would happen after that can be described in the words of the lecturer himself, who wrote:

On receipt, the specimen would be divided into halves. One half would be deep frozen under special conditions and kept indefinitely. The other half would be examined with respect to (1) the histology of the integument; (2) the chromosome complement; and (3) antigen specificity, much as the forensic experts identify a fragment of tissue as human, or dog etc.

Each one of these three examinations is capable of identifying the species, or at least indicating that the species is one not previously recognized as extant. The deep frozen half would be kept in reserve for further analysis if required.

Realizing that the method of recovering the specimen from the probe was now an important matter, I set about devising a means of withdrawing it whole. With so many barbs to contend with, it could not be taken out the same way as it went in without damage – so I machined a small hole in the brass plug mounting the skewer, and tapped a 6 BA thread in it. Next I made up a key to screw into it, which would enable me to extract the skewer and specimen from the rear of the coring head; this was set into the fishing float and attached to the arrow shaft internally. Once removed, like a worm on a fish-hook, the specimen could be slit down one side with a razor blade, and stripped from the skewer and barbs without further injury. A slit down the other side would then provide the two identical sections needed.

It is often surprising how one event or introduction can lead to another, which in turn leads to something else. After talking to the expert in hypo-darting at Cambridge, I came to the conclusion that attempting to tranquillize the Monster, as a means of defence or research was not practical, because the animal species and the individual weight must be known if the drug is to be measured out effectively. If this is not done there is a risk of either killing the beast or stimulating it . . . and the idea of a stimulated 'Nessie' at close quarters did not appeal to me. Besides, the drug, which looked like Stephens ink, was so dangerous to man it could only be used with a veterinary or medical doctor in attendance.

But the interview put me on to another person who was an electronics expert working for the Medical Research Council in London, Mr H. S. Wolff BSC, who was concerned with the design of tiny transmitter systems for recording the human heartbeat at a distance.

I was interested in the possibility of firing into the Monster a transmitting dart which could then be followed from shore-based tracking stations. I doubted if this was really practical, but wanted to discuss the matter with someone who had experience.

As expected, it was feasible as a technical exercise, but there were problems which would rule it out in practice – unless someone was prepared to devote a lot of time and money to it. I was not;

but something came out of the discussion which promised to be useful.

One of the developments with which Mr Wolff was concerned was the rocket launching of a distress transmitter aerial from an RAF dinghy – giving the aircrew, who had been forced to ditch in the sea, a better chance of being heard on radio. He told me of a startling breakthrough in hand-held rocketry, and put me on to a small firm which was concerned with it, and with the development of illuminating flares and other pyrotechnics.

Realizing the potential value of parachute flares for use in night photography I asked to be given an introduction to one of the directors, because the firm did not cater to the public in the ordinary commercial sense. Its products were used by the armed services, and by the Coastguard and Royal National Lifeboat Institution, though kits of distress signals were sold through dealers to the yachting fraternity.

This was arranged, and in due course I met the sales director who laid on a demonstration of flares, signals, line-throwing rockets and other ingenious devices which quite fascinated me. I found a friend in the demonstrator too. There is a particular breed of people who are drawn towards pyrotechnics, who recognize in each other a common trait. They love bangs, and stars and clouds of coloured smoke, and as small boys, are sometimes found making black powder bombs, with which to sabotage other people's duck ponds. They are essentially pyrotechnic-types.

The demonstration started with a bang, as I was shown a device known as the Mini-Flare Pack. This was a pocket-size red plastic kit containing a row of coloured flares, which screwed into a spring-loaded firing projector. It produced a star ascending a hundred feet or so, much like a Verey cartridge pistol. It was intended for yachtsmen, or small-boat people, and could be carried underwater by skin divers who could loose one off if they came up a long way from their boat.

A blinding 20,000 candle-power hand flare was next on the list; I was allowed to hold it, and became enveloped in a fine white ash and clouds of billowing smoke. It was impressive, but not so exciting as a hand-held rocket maroon, sizzling upwards to explode at 1,200 ft with a noise like dynamite. The next test hung a 100,000 candle-power parachute flare in the sky, drifting slowly down leaving a trail of smoke.

Other items were shown, and with each performance the *bonhomie* increased, reaching a peak when an enormous firework, known as a 'Flash, Sound and Trace Signal' was let off.

As far as I could judge, this was fired by 'Trinity House Light Vessels' to wake up the captains of coastal vessels who were either too tired or too tipsy to notice that they were heading for the rocks! The demonstration produced an object about the size of a thermos flask shooting upwards, exploding in the air with a gigantic flash and thunderous percussion which shook the earth, and echoed round the county.

It was, without question, a most satisfying afternoon. We retired from the field of action and later I made a number of useful purchases. I had also made some friends.

5
Chasm of Glenmore

On Friday, 30 August 1968 we loaded up our expedition car, an old Mark 8 Jaguar, in preparation for the journey north. As a last-minute precaution, I got in touch with an acquaintance who worked for the British Aluminium Company at Fort William, and he agreed to act as link-man in the event of something going wrong on the journey up, either with *Cizara* or the Jaguar, putting his phone at our disposal for this purpose.

We left Reading early and headed east to pick up the Great North Road, connecting London with Edinburgh. It has been much improved in recent years and I knew the car would cover the 330 miles to my brother's farm in Northumberland in a matter of hours.

It would have been simpler to travel up alone, but I wanted the family to participate in what could be a real adventure, the journey up through the Caledonian Canal into Loch Ness.

Arriving at Newcastle-upon-Tyne we drove the remaining few miles to the farm, deep in the countryside, and climbed out to greet my brother's family, and the pet animals, which are part of it.

On Sunday we set off once more, waving goodbye, and drove up through the Cheviot Hills, crossing the Scottish border and stopping to view the sweeping panorama which lay to the north. Instead of continuing to Edinburgh we swung left, driving through Selkirk and Peeblesshire, on to Glasgow and Loch Lomond, where we stopped again to stretch our legs and eat a hurried sandwich. Time was slipping by. I had agreed to meet *Cizara* off the pier at Fort William at approximately half past six, but with the narrow winding roads it was difficult to average more than 30 m.p.h.

At Ballachulish Ferry, entrance to the sea loch, Loch Leven, we joined a queue of vehicles waiting to board and cross the tidal narrows – and as it was now 7 p.m. I phoned the house in Fort

William, hoping to leave a message. Ominously there was no reply. I realized we would be more than two hours late, but there was nothing I could do about it, and waited a turn at the ferry, the children crunching remorselessly through bags of potato crisps.

Arriving at Fort William, we drove down the coastal road, and straight towards the pier, which extends into the salt water of Loch Linnhe. Boats were at anchor, but there was no sign of *Cizara*.

To make absolutely certain, I walked down to a railway siding and climbed a hummock of ground to peer over the top of a long commercial jetty, gaining a view of the northern end of the loch. I could see fishing vessels in the distance, and a village at the entrance to Loch Eil, extending westwards – but the distinctive twin hulls of *Cizara* were nowhere in evidence.

My heart sank, and I slowly lowered the binoculars. She must have engine trouble, and would be lying becalmed, perhaps 30 miles down the coast.

We had nowhere to stay, we were tired and irritable, and had been counting on an evening meal aboard. For a moment I wished we were all back at home. There was no boat in sight, and that was that!

I wondered if there could be a hidden entrance basin to the Caledonian Ship Canal. It seemed unlikely but we made an abortive attempt to find it, driving through Fort William and making inquiries. We drove round in circles, and then as a last resort decided to return to the house we had passed on the way to Fort William, where my friend from the Aluminium Company lived.

Arriving ten minutes later I strode up to the door and knocked. There was no reply, but on turning to leave I noticed a scrap of paper stuck to the woodwork. I opened it to find a cryptic note: 'Would Mr Dinsdale please go round to the back door where he would find instructions in an envelope pinned to the door-post.'

Feeling like someone on a treasure hunt I made my way round to the back, crunching over the gravel, suppressing a desire to run. I found the envelope, and inside it a sheet of notepaper. Ian Smith had waited for us, before taking *Cizara* round to the canal basin at Corpach. He included careful instructions on how to get there. I walked back to the car with measured tread, viewing the row of anxious faces.

Turning left outside Fort William, I drove northwards looking for landmarks – and noticed the weather was deteriorating. Dark clouds heavy with rain were approaching from the south; the light was failing too and I did not look forward to shuttling aboard in the dinghy. I guessed it would take an hour or so at least.

Finding a side-road and scarcely legible sign, we turned down towards the basin at Corpach, which proved to be a deserted wharf with one or two outbuildings, and a large crane standing gaunt against the skyline. We rounded another bend – and there, almost in front of us was *Cizara* tied up alongside, immaculate and gleaming white. The effect was startling.

I parked the car a foot or two from her, and with the first large spots of rain pattering on the water we fitted the tent tarpaulin over the cockpit, and handled the more essential items down. But then it started to rain in torrents and within perhaps one minute of our getting safely aboard, the heavens opened and drenched the surrounding countryside.

It poured all night in a never-ending drumfire on the roof, but we were snug inside, and after a meal the family tucked itself up to spend a first night peacefully asleep aboard the elusive catamaran, which had for so long plagued my imagination.

In December of the previous year I had written to Frank and Constance Whyte in Sussex, retired from their long association with the Caledonian Ship Canal, which Mr Whyte had run as manager. One of the first jobs in costing-out *Makita* was to establish the dues and procedure necessary to take a large yacht through the waterway. I was put on to a Mr R. B. Davenport, the new Manager, at Clachnaharry, Inverness. He posted me a set of documents which listed toll charges and the facilities available. I could not have asked for a more efficient service. At that time on Loch Ness there was only one usable 'primitive' wooden pier, and a few private mooring buoys on Loch Dochfour, at the north-eastern extremity – but to tie up to these would require permission in advance.

It was not an encouraging prospect, and with insecure deep-water anchorage as an alternative I was glad of the promise, given me by the monks at St Benedict's Abbey, at Fort Augustus, to allow

Cizara to tie up close inshore near their boathouse. I had no idea if this was a protected spot but decided to take the Jaguar to the Abbey by road, and find out, as a first move on 2 September, when we awoke to a tranquil morning on the pondlike surface of the basin.

The weather was dull but it had stopped raining, and we got on with the task of unloading the car. The night had passed uneventfully with Ian Smith sleeping on the cockpit deck in a camp bed, under the weather-proof tarpaulin, and the children disposed inside. Simon and Alexandra, the two eldest were in the port and starboard forward bunks, and Dawn and Angus between them in a double bunk. My wife, Wendy, and I slept on the seats to the folding table. We had all been comfortable, if a little cramped. Meals were served amidships, with hot plates of food passing directly from the galley – at a pinch we could sit four a side at the table. It was a cheerful gathering.

Ian Smith had offered to accompany me to Fort Augustus in his own car so that I would not have to bus back. The journey by road was just over 30 miles. We arrived at the Abbey together, after a scenic drive through the mountainous countryside, and made contact with Fr Aloysius Carruth, the Scottish monk I had first met in 1960.

He took us round to the back of the Abbey, an extensive grey stone building, and down to the water's edge, which was shut off from view by trees and the boathouse. But, more importantly, a jetty wall perhaps 6 to 8 ft high ran out protecting a small area of water, like a miniature harbour. An old clinker-built longboat, with a mast, was tied up to the jetty, and beneath her lay the remains of a sunken metal barge.

A quick glance told us that here was a sheltered spot with access to the shore. In all the years I had been working at Loch Ness I had never realized the potential value of the boathouse wall. Indeed, I had scarcely noticed it because it was only visible from the water, or the south shore road high up on the mountainside.

Back at the basin, we made arrangements for departure. Ian had already been to the local canal office to pay the dues, and the keeper came round to see us off. He brought an enormous St Bernard dog

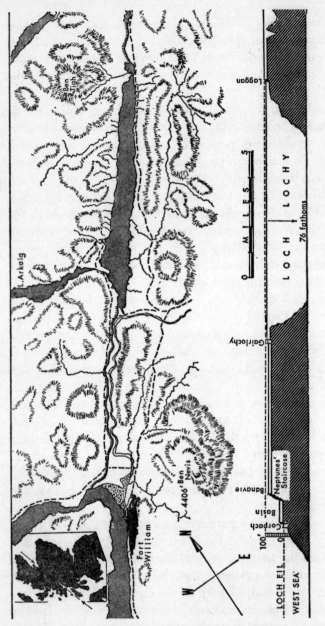

Figure 4   Caledonian Ship Canal System (western section)

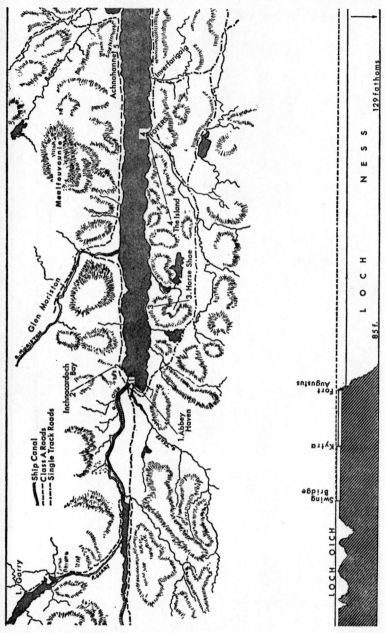

Figure 5   Caledonian Ship Canal System (central section)
E

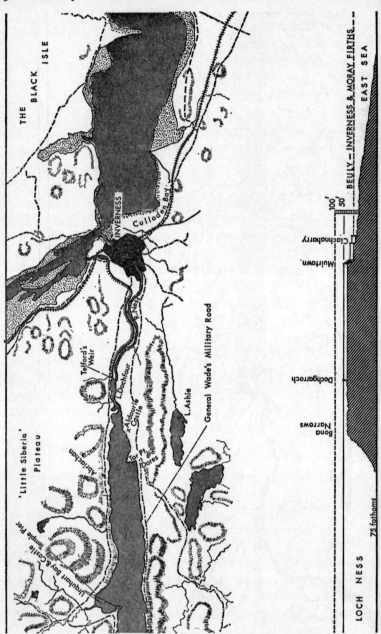

Figure 6   Caledonian Ship Canal System (eastern section)

which gazed at us with friendly brown eyes. One got the impression the two were inseparable.

The canal exit had been quiet when *Cizara* was tied up there, and with the exception of one blunt-nosed trawler nothing had moved through the massive locks, which extended eight in a row eastwards. Banavie locks, better known as 'Neptune's Staircase', lifting vessels 80 ft above high water mark.

Our British Waterways chart folder, showing the canal system both in plan and section, stated that: 'Vessels will save circum-navigation of, and find safe and commodious passage across, the Island of Great Britain, from the Moray Firth to Loch Linnhe, by the Caledonian Canal, which commences at Clachnaharry, near Inverness, and terminates at Corpach, near Fort William.'

It also explained that 'vessels of up to 160 feet in length and 36 feet in the beam can use the canal, which is fresh, with a minimum depth of 14 feet' – and that the 'passage from Sea to Sea is sixty miles'. Maps and charts had always interested me, but there was something quaint about the folder.

At 13.35 hours, as noted in the log, we started the outboard engine and moved into the first cavernous lock, the massive wooden gates inching to behind us. With ropes secured to bollards fore and aft *Cizara* rose gently on the flood. We eased her up, keeping her close to the wall, slimy with lichens and verdigris. It was cold and dank, and a patter of rain made the decks slippery. It was tedious work, but with each lock *Cizara* rose gently until we could see the countryside about us. To the south, Ben Nevis, rising 4,406 feet, was lost in the clouds, and the mossy greens and browns of the Highlands blended together, softened by the intervening mist.

Perhaps an hour later we cleared the final lock, and, waving good-bye to the keeper, moved out into the channel. The canal and its lock-gate system gave one the impression of an age of unhurried, gracious progression past sweeping willows, and ancient sluice gates stained with emerald moss. With the engine throttled down to burbling, we cruised gently along, conscious of the peace – the occasional liquid birdsong trilling in accompaniment.

For the next 6 or 7 miles *Cizara* meandered along the waterway, a river flowing past in the valley below and the mountains rising to either side. At Moy, we passed under the first swing bridge, and at Gairlochy a second, with traffic held up on either side. Beyond, another pair of lock gates lifted the boat 10 ft to the surface of Loch Lochy stretching 12 miles to the east.

We sailed through at leisurely pace, past Glenfintaig and Invergloy and Letterfinlay and Glastard, names on the map marking a lonely mansion house, partly obscured by trees, or a group of crofters' dwellings – stupendous scenery, with Ben Tigh emerging from the mists like a giant.

About mid-way we served tea, then discussed the best plan of sailing. There was no rush. In time the weather would improve, and we still had four days of sailing ahead, with everyone on board. We decided to drop anchor, and moved forward to the bow deck. I watched the anchor plummet into the water, then dive away at an angle, trailing its chain just like an aerial kite.

The time was after 6 p.m., and with rain clouds building up once more we rigged the tent tarpaulin over the cockpit, and peered at the barometer. It seemed to have stuck in the 'wet and windy' position.

Early next morning with condensation dripping off the cabin roof I tapped it again. The pointer moved to indicate a small improvement, and by the time *Cizara* weighed anchor it was reading 'cloudy, dry, mild and calm'. This had a cheering effect on the crew, and I knew from experience on expeditions that morale and the barometer tended to go up and down together.

With more locks and another swing bridge behind us we sailed into Loch Oich, studying the chart which carried the warning: 'Loch Oich is buoyed and beaconed, and care must be exercised in navigating.' At 100 ft above sea level *Cizara* was now on the highest section of the canal, but of the three Great Glen lochs, Loch Oich is the smallest, and by comparison with its neighbours no more than a puddle in depth.

We entered it, counting off the buoys which marked the channel. In character, too, it was different, with low wooded scenery to our left and the dramatic old ruin of Invergarry Castle. To the right mountains rose steeply to 1,000 ft, then more gradually to twice that height in a series of craggy escarpments.

We lingered on the four-mile passage, and I shot film, listening to the even purr of the camera mechanism. Loch Oich – the 'place of awe' is a masterpiece of nature. It seemed a pity to leave it.

Back in the canal, another swing bridge held up the motor traffic, and with a feeling of self-consciousness we drifted through, coiling ropes and performing other minor tasks. At 11.15 a.m., *Cizara* came on the first set of locks descending towards the east. Going downhill was easier, and pleasantly sedate, and with the first hint of sunlight shining through the mist we set off on this final leg of the journey – the canal wandering off close to a river, which flowed gently by in a broad shallow stream towards Loch Ness.

6
Fabled waters of the Ness

Approaching Loch Ness for the very first time in April 1960, I had taken the south shore road from Inverness. It was late evening, and I was tired after a day at the wheel, but anticipating my first view of the fabulous lake I had read so much about and studied so carefully. At a point roughly a mile from the village of Dores, at the eastern extremity, the road abruptly puts one in view of the water and the jagged panorama of mountains. In the gloom of evening the sheen of afterlight upon the water threw the whole scene into relief, and when I stopped the car and climbed out of it I was aware of the tingle up my spine, and a curious breathlessness. It was as though I was standing in the field of an enormous electro-magnet, which took control of me, drawing me irresistibly forwards. A strange, almost fearful compulsion – but with it a feeling of familiarity.

I was unable to explain this, because I was not a person who felt that 'he had been there before', and I would tend to discount such feelings on the basis of coincidence. But this was altogether different. I had never been there before, and yet I knew it. The dark and mysteriously beautiful scene was entirely foreign to me, and yet I recognized it.

Oddly enough, subsequent visits to the loch, approaching from the east, but on the north shore road, did not produce this effect, though it was always repeatable on the south shore road; and as I found out the year following, at the western approaches too. Driving towards Fort Augustus from the west along the motor road, a point is reached where the aspect is altogether different, because Loch Ness is first seen as a giant cleft in the mountains, long before the water comes into view. This view had precisely the same effect on me – and approaching from the canal in the valley bottom a mile distant from the road, I wondered just how I would react, and how it would affect the others.

Once through the Kytra locks the sun came out, and I climbed on to the cabin roof to train with the camera. I was getting the feel of it, but when no more than half a mile from Fort Augustus I heard a change of note in the camera motor, and within seconds the gate mechanism jammed up, a high pitched futile whine coming from the magazine.

With a mild convulsion in the pit of my stomach, I climbed down and went into the cabin. The camera was new, and special tests had been carried out to prove its reliability. The magazine alone had cost £100. And yet, at the very point of entry to Loch Ness it had failed!

I retreated under a blanket, and slipped it into a changing bag. The scenery could go to hell – unless I could fix it quickly I would enter the Ness with a defective movie camera and thus act out the details of a recurrent dream which had troubled me for years, in which the Beast would surface only yards away. When this happened my camera was always defective. It was a silly dream, but all the same, I worked as fast as I could in the dark, using my finger-tips as sensors. For some reason the drive to the magazine take-up spool had failed. I removed the 200-ft spool and put in one of half the size in the camera body itself. It was a poor alternative and meant I had only two minutes of actual filming time. But I was no longer without a 16mm camera.

Back on deck I could see we were almost on top of Fort Augustus; quite literally, we were looking over the roof tops, and the towers of St Benedict's Abbey. Another staircase of five locks stepped down through the centre of the village, and under a road-bridge – a drop in water level of roughly 40 ft.

Two other vessels lay ahead, waiting for us in the confines of the lock. Things seemed brighter now, with sunlight and colour, and crowds of spectators in holiday mood.

It took an hour to work *Cizara* through the locks, but we were down by 1.30 p.m. and motored gently out of the canal and round to the Abbey jetty, tying up there, next to the derelict longboat *Narwhal*. The weather was good and the barometer ascending.

Eating lunch, we decided to remain tied up for the day, then set off early next morning. The girls would go ashore to shop in Fort Augustus, while Ian Smith and I checked over the equipment.

With the family back on board we spent a comfortable night and at 11.50 a.m. next day cast off and backed out slowly from the jetty. With the rudders hard over, *Cizara* made way, heading eastwards up the loch.

Part two of the adventure had now really begun.

At midday, under the faintest suspicion of a breeze, we put the sails up and moved forward beneath the towering rock-wall of the southern shore. I had so often gazed across the loch at this mysterious precipice. Its remoteness seemed to hold the key to something, and when 2 or 3 miles of it had passed, across from Point Clair – or 'Gobhar Sgiathach', to give it a name in Gaelic – something peculiar happened, so peculiar that Ian Smith who kept *Cizara*'s log with all the care of a professional sailor made a note of it. He wrote: 'Saw ripples travelling South to North, about ten inches high.'

He did not make this entry to please me, or at my suggestion, because when on board he was the skipper. What interested him was the fact that no boats were in sight; the wind, too, which was scarcely strong enough to create a surface ripple, was blowing from the opposite direction. The ripples could not be explained, and they were impressive. A 10-in pattern moving contrary to the wind, apparently caused by something large moving through the water.

After a long, slow journey eastwards the sails came down and we motored to drop anchor for the night close to Foyers Point. The weather was holding, and the night passed uneventfully. I awoke to a mist-enshrouded morning with the water oily calm. The habit of rising early at Loch Ness was difficult to break, and with the family still in their bunks I stepped into the dinghy and rowed off to take some photographs. *Cizara* looked ghostly in the mist with the sun shining through it like a silver medallion.

Before long a verbal exchange developed across the water. I could not resist shouting encouragement to those inside the yacht, then rapping on the hull, lying comfortably back in the little boat, paddling about with my hands. Muffled sounds made it clear I should move back out of range – and as the sun burned away the mist, life aboard *Cizara* became more evident.

We breakfasted, then tidied ship before pulling up the sails. With the wind abeam, sailing on a broad reach, *Cizara* gained speed, and for the first time the twin white wakes developed. We tilted the motor clear of the water, then turned east going nicely, perhaps 100 yards from shore, gazed at by motorists. Before long we passed by the LNPIB main camera site some 200 ft above, at Achnahannet. The crew had spotted us further down the loch and waved.

Urquhart Castle next hove into sight and we had a fine view of the ruin from the water. The wind was freshening now and, turning, we crossed the broadest expanse of the loch, heading for Dores, going about opposite the village at 1.20 p.m. It was not quite the eastern extremity, because the loch divides on both sides of Tor Point, a lonely outcrop of glacial stones and boulders, but it was as far as we could go towards the south shore.

Cizara began to pitch, and with spray flying we tacked back and forth at speed. It was intoxicating, and for the first time I tried my hand at sailing her alone.

By now Angus, the youngest member of the crew had lost his *joie de vivre*, and retired below to sit with his arms round his mother, who was also looking pallid. In order not to spoil the day we ran for shelter, dropping anchor in Urquhart Bay half an hour later.

It is a large bay, with a delta area to the north combining the efflux from two small rivers flowing through it – a lonely, wooded patch of land, where the Beast was reported to have been seen out of water many years before.

That evening, swinging at anchor we played games, and told stories. The two younger children had shown signs of nervousness, the Monster looming large in their imagination. I knew there was a chance of meeting it in Urquhart Bay, because the sonar work done by Birmingham University during the two weeks previously had shown large objects rising at speed from a depth of 600 ft, moving in and out of the beam. Their base for operations was at Temple Pier, just half a mile away.

Retiring late we dozed off to the rattle and bump of the anchor chain. Squalls of wind came whistling down the glen, striking *Cizara*, which reacted with a shudder. Lights on the mountainside blinked through the cabin windows as she pirouetted round.

Up at 6 a.m. next morning I hauled the anchor, by inches – it seemed immensely heavy, bringing with it an old decaying tree trunk around which the chain had wound itself during the windstorms of the night. It must have doubled our security.

It was a fine morning, and we left under motor, steering past Urquhart Castle. While breakfasting, we took turns at the wheel and in due time Fort Augustus came into view, the towers of St Benedict's slowly getting bigger until we could make out details in the stonework. Tying up to *Narwhal* we stepped ashore on to the jetty to gaze back up the loch to the dim horizon. It was such a lovely, natural place – and we had just been through an experience not one of us would forget.

Later that afternoon, motoring over to pay another call to Achnahannet I met two young men who claimed a Monster sighting from the Altsaigh youth hostel, at roughly the same time we had logged the ripples; and almost opposite. They were excited, having seen a hump and a great V-wash in the water. By now the sun had set, and on the trip back to Fort Augustus, approaching Inchnacardoch Bay with its tiny island in the middle – Cherry Island, we had a sighting ourselves. It was only momentary, and took us completely by surprise, but there could be little doubt about it.

Approaching the bay from behind the screen of firs, we abruptly came in sight of the water. The six passengers all saw something, and said 'What's that?' I was looking ahead, driving, and by the time I had glanced round the screen of trees was springing up again – I just caught a glimpse of the water, and Cherry Island with its clump of tall conifers, but I knew the shallow water of the bay had produced inshore sightings in the past, and clapped on the brakes.

We stopped, and clutching the binoculars (it was too late for photography) my son and I raced back to clear the trees. It must have taken us 20 or 30 seconds: but there was nothing to be seen. No sound either, of an outboard motor boat.

During the remaining five-minute drive back to Fort Augustus,

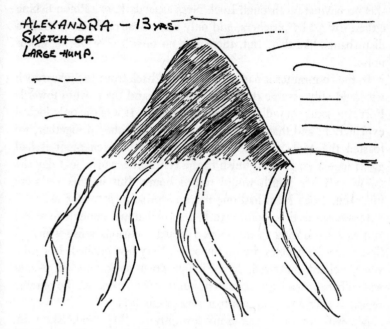

ALEXANDRA — 13 YRS.
SKETCH OF
LARGE HUMP.

Figure 7   Alexandra's sketch of large hump

I questioned the witnesses closely. They had all seen something big, moving away, and leaving a wake. My wife thought it might have been a rowing boat with the pointed bow creating the impression of a hump, but the two girls and Angus said it *was* a hump. Ian Smith had naturally concluded it was a boat, because of its size, but Simon who had exceptional eyesight said it was the Monster. But whatever it may have been, it could not have been a boat, because in 20–30 seconds it could not have simply disappeared.

Back at the Abbey, I parked the Jaguar, then chatted with Ian Smith while the others made their way down to the jetty wall. We followed them and there, rolling in from the black, oily calm surface of the loch were the astonishing waves we had seen before, over-taking the yacht. The girls were excited, and said they had been much bigger before our arrival, breaking on the shore; and sweeping round the jetty wall to rock *Cizara* at her moorings.

There was no ordinary explanation for this disturbance. There was no navigation through Loch Ness after dark, or salmon fishing either, except by poachers, and only a big boat could have made a disturbance like that. But, there was no breath of wind, or motor noise.

In the 10 minutes it had taken us to get back from Inchnacardoch we could only assume the Beast had dived and then swum towards Fort Augustus, rounding the end of the loch. It was the only logical explanation, and that night which was our last aboard together, we toasted the Monster, glad of the moments of excitement it had given us – a grandstand finish to the venture, because next day the 'crew' and Mr Smith would return home. But in this we were mistaken. Loch Ness had one more surprise in store for us.

It was some time before we had settled down enough to sleep, and as I lay dozing in my bunk I heard a curious noise which at first made the hackles rise on my scalp. Very low pitched, I heard a voice, a chant, muttered, unintelligible words spoken in a sing-song way. There was an ugly tone to it, but it was purposeful, the phrases repeated over and over, approaching gradually.

My wife sat up in her bunk apruptly . . . 'My God,' she said, 'what's that?' as with a crash from the rotting deck of *Narwhal* a pair of human legs leapt aboard. I could see them through the cabin window. I sat bolt upright too, and flicked on the light.

Scrabbling sounds, and another lurch took the owner of the legs back on to the jetty, but he stood there just long enough for me to glimpse a tall thin man who turned unsteadily to glance back over his shoulder, before disappearing into the night.

It was an unpleasant incident, and it spoiled the feeling of security gained at the little harbour. For the next two weeks I would be alone there at night on a valuable piece of property which belonged to someone else – *Cizara*.

Fortunately, the children had slept through it, and departed next day unruffled, looking forward to the long journey home by train. I watched the car drive off up the lane with mixed feelings; sorry to see them go and yet glad to be alone once more, to face the loch, and the tasks which lay ahead. I would miss their joyous company, and yet I was relieved of the responsibility. But above all I was grateful for the experience we had enjoyed so much together.

7
Letter home

Aboard *Cizara*,
Ft. Augustus,
Loch Ness.
Saturday, Sept 14th 1968

I thought you would like to know how things are progressing. . . .

When you left on Saturday morning last, I must say after all the noise and activity and squash aboard I felt pretty lonely, and the slow process of getting things into some sort of order was started without much enthusiasm. I decided to stay at the quayside – or rather tied up at the Abbey Haven, which is what I now call it. For some reason I was feeling tired too, and kept knocking off for a stretch out on the bunk. On Sunday, these stretch outs became a necessity, because I began to feel most peculiar. A thumping headache, and a curious lassitude, just as though I'd been dipped in treacle; it was a huge effort to do anything at all. On previous expeditions I have noticed this – perhaps a sort of physical boomerang to all the weeks of preparation – and worrying about equipment and forgetting things etc., only this time it was worse.

However, by Monday I'd got over it and the long job of dressing *Cizara* in her camouflage skirt was done, and very satisfactorily too. These long sections of old sheeting dyed and painted in blobs are tailored to the hull on either side exactly, and suspended by lengths of sisal string. The brilliant white of the hull would certainly catch Nessie's eye if she has any sort of vision at all.

Another job, which turned out well was the simple idea for a dark room. I draped the old blue bed cover over the windows in the toilet, and although of course it doesn't keep out all the light, it's subdued enough now for me to change films.

Regarding the very unwelcome 'boarder' we had last Friday night – I mentioned this to Fr. Aloysius. . . . I think the tuneless singing we heard was a ruse to see if anyone was about. When there was no response, the man decided to come on deck to find if there was anything worth lifting. I told Fr. Aloysius I would not allow anyone to come aboard Ian's yacht without permission, and meant it – and he quite agreed – but in the interests of preserving the peace should a second attempt be made, at night I string a long line and pull *Cizara* out into the water. Anyone who wants to board her in future will have to swim first before receiving a large biff on the nose – but there's been no trouble since.

On Monday afternoon, I decided to make a sortie, but when I went to start the engine – grr grr and then nothing. The battery was flat. I had to start it by hand – which was quite hard work, as it has a very high compression. I got away all right and cruised around for a bit, experiencing that mixture of elation and anxiety which is a part of every first solo performance – be it in an aeroplane, on a pushbike or a pair of roller skates. . . . A small naval vessel went by towards the Caledonian, and paid attention through binoculars. I felt very 'lone sailorish' and toyed with the idea of dipping the Ensign – only I'd forgotten to put it up.

It was quite calm and after buzzing about to bump up the battery, I nosed gingerly into Cherry Island Bay, where you all got your Monster sighting on Friday night, sounding out the bottom on the fathometer. There were a few boats and yachts moored there, next to a pier, quite obviously in use (which is the exception on L.N.) so I guessed there must be a good anchorage. The machine showed ten feet under the hull. I should think it is the best anchorage on the Ness.

I got back with some difficulty as there was a side wind, and I over corrected and missed the first approach. As you know, this is a safe little harbour, but there is no room to spare sideways between the main protecting jetty and the partly completed one, sticking out towards it from the opposite shore. Anyway, I made it and felt much better.

On Monday night there was a brilliant steely moonlight, and I awoke to the screech of a Loch Ness squall in the rigging. The shore ropes were bow string tight, and dear old broken-down *Narwhal* with her crazy bowsprit askew, cavorted back and forth clinking her piles of rusted chain. *Cizara*, not to be outdone, joined in the dance, a kind of minuet it seemed to me, bobbing back and forth sometimes in harmony, and sometimes out of step. To and fro they went, obviously enjoying it. I watched until two in the morning then dozed off, to a dull and cloudy morning with a tinge of pink in the sky.

I got on with the chores, then I tried the engine again. It barely turned over on the starter, then refused to do any more ... so I started it by hand.

I set off with misgivings. The wind was rising, and I knew if I stopped the engine I would probably have to start it by hand, and if it didn't go – I might drift on to the lonely rock-lined shore before I could get the sails up: allowing twenty minutes to do this for a single-hander.

About 2 miles out I stopped, and began to drift about. The water was black like ink with the heavy overcast, but with patches of intense ripple on it, like vibration ripples almost; it looked sinister and I found the boat drifted along at two or three knots without any sail at all. Another curious thing – for some obscure reason, due perhaps to the unusual light the vast sheet of water seemed slightly convex – like the meniscus (or is it miniscus) on a tube of mercury. I decided to try and start the motor, just to see if it would go ... and when it did, on the button, I was so relieved I found the boat heading straight for home and safety with me holding the wheel. But it wouldn't do. I had a lot of things to test, so I stopped the damn thing again.

On Wednesday I left the Haven before breakfast, and went out to the Horse Shoe. It was a mist-enshrouded morning, with the water flat calm. I let go of the helm and drifted about becalmed for six hours without touching it. Before me the loch stretched to the horizon, with the mountains draped in swaths of mist. Not a boat or a human being in sight – just the gigantic sheet of jelly with weird reflections on it, and *Cizara* alone on the surface.

On Thursday by contrast, I set off and motored up to Foyers in a blustery wind, with whitecaps everywhere. It was just like being out at sea. I got there at 2 p.m., scouted the bay, then went out to the exact place on the water where I saw the Beast in 1960. I wanted to see what a human being would look like on the little road high up on the south shore, at the place where I had been that eventful morning. A sort of 'Nessie's eye view' so to speak.

Shutting down the motor, I turned to drift home, a distance of about 12 miles. *Cizara* made three knots on the log, heaving up and down gently like a great big rocking-horse. There were whitecaps as far as I could see, and the magnificent scenery bright in the sunlight. What a wonderful experience!

At first the boat yawed from side to side, but surprisingly, I found I could control her on the rudders and tack her as though she had sail up . . . only without the mad scramble of going about. Sailing without sails, in fact!

And so all the way back to the wee harbour in about four hours; but here I ran into trouble. Trying to squeeze in I was broadside to the wind. *Cizara* drifted sideways to within inches of the rocks. It gave me a real fright, believe me. But I made it on the next attempt and leapt ashore to do battle with the ropes. Don't ask me how I won the tug of war, because the wind force was terrific and the catamaran nearly pulled me into the harbour.

Curiously enough on the way in that day I had a presentiment of danger – of something going wrong; and the need not to venture out on Friday. Quite obviously unless the wind died down I couldn't, but it was also to be Friday the 13th which as any sailor knows is a good enough excuse.

In the morning as the wind was still blowing I went ashore. On the way up to the Abbey I met Fr. Aloysius, who told me Dawn had been taken to hospital with a suspected appendicitis. . . .

The last week of the expedition was fraught with anxiety about my daughter's health. At first I spent as much time ashore phoning home as I did aboard *Cizara*, but as Dawn's mysterious illness took its course, and her temperature came down a decision was taken to postpone the operation – which relieved me of the need to catch a sleeper home, and tie up the catamaran. I was glad not to have to do this because with no one aboard to repel intruders at night she could have been stripped of equipment.

Another problem had arisen too, which caused the Smiths anxiety. The Crinan Canal was due to close for repairs, and unless *Cizara* could be taken out through it the following weekend she would be forced to sail round the Kintyre peninsula, adding a hundred nautical miles to the journey, and exposing her to the risk of winter gales on this dangerous coastline.

But in spite of everything, the days remaining on Loch Ness were full of experience, and I gained more confidence in handling the boat. I could not ignore the fantastic beauties surrounding me, the mists of early morning and the silence, enveloping and spiritual.

At times I found it hard to believe I was still in the twentieth century, living on the Planet Earth – I seemed to be floating in another-worldly paradise, another dimension, without time, or material content.

But these effects were transient, and I would be brought back to reality by a mechanical failure, or the wind, and the urgent need to control the boat.

Since the discovery of driftsailing, which was accidental, I had been able to move *Cizara* about downwind without a stitch of canvas. She could be tacked on the rudders, and at first I was at a loss to explain this because it worked right down the windscale to a speed of half a knot.

Ultimately, I came to the conclusion the mast was acting like a glider's wing – a low speed aerofoil of high aspect ratio which produced a horizontal lift component; a wing which enabled me to 'fly' the cat. using the big plate rudders for control. It saved me the trouble of putting up sails as I could simply motor upwind, then driftsail back again. The wind usually blew one way or the other up and down the loch due to the funnelling effect; and it was this effect which produced the whiplash squalls, and the high wind velocities. The walls of Loch Ness formed a 'venturi' which accelerated the wind at the narrow places.

Driftsailing had another advantage too, because I was not in truth a yachtsman, and could not even begin to understand *Bill O'Brien's 8 Metre Handling and Check Notes for Owners*. In every sport there

F

is an element of jargon, and as sailing must be one of the oldest and most historic sports, the jargon has developed to the point where it is unintelligible to all but the enthusiast. Section Three of *The Check Notes for Owners* reads as follows:

> *a* 'Bend' the mainsail to the boom by sliding the foot thro'
> the groove from the gooseneck end.
> *b* Connect gooseneck shackle to tack of sail eye cringle.
> *c* Pull clew to sail out to boom end, and lash securely to outhall,
> yet leaving some cord for two turns around boom through
> clew cringle.
> *d* Insert sail battens in pockets . . . avoid puckering of sail
> leach. . . .
> *e* Connect halyard to head of sail using 'D' shackle . . . running
> free and clear of spreaders.
> *f* Insert mainsail luff slides in mast groove . . . etc.

Inexorably, as the hunt drew to a close I became aware that my dream-world existence would finish, and that all the cares and burdens of modern life would again take its place. But before this happened one other curious event occurred. On 19 September a large white-painted work-vessel moved into the loch, attended by a powerful inflated boat from the shore. She was called the *Prince Maddog*, and displaced several hundred tons. The crew appeared to be involved in research work of some kind, dumping a probe, or sonar device over the side. I steered clear of her, feeling that if it was a 'pinger' I would be better away from it.

On the day following, with a gale whipping up the waters, *Cizara* remained tied up at the Abbey jetty until the Smiths arrived. That night I stripped the equipment and stowed it in the Jaguar, which I had moved down to the jetty. I also lowered my little wind-blown pennant from the mast-head, and at 7.10 a.m. next morning *Cizara* let go fore and aft, and moved off.

I stood on the jetty and waved. She looked different in her decamouflaged paint – but the Smiths were in a hurry, and she soon disappeared into the entrance of the canal. I was in a hurry too, because I wanted to get home to see my daughter, who was still in hospital recovering from the fever.

For a moment I stood gazing out once more over the vast expanse of water, at ancient, friendly *Narwhal*, quietly rotting at her moorings. The scene was one of unutterable loneliness – and peace. The Great Loch had retained its secret, but I had no feelings of resentment. We had done our best, and had been rewarded with a living, colourful experience, the memory of which would never fade.

Turning, I climbed into the big car and drove the long miles home almost without stopping, arriving late that night.

The next day Dawn came home, pale and wan and very, very serious, and when she had recovered her strength sufficiently she had her appendix removed. I sat up with her all night at the hospital, feeling it would comfort her and make up for my absence when circumstances had made things so difficult.

Slowly, our lives returned to normal. The children went back to school and Simon, our eldest boy, left home to join the Royal Armoured Corps.

It was several weeks, however, before I could get an uninterrupted night. I kept getting up in my sleep and moving to the window to check the weather, and the ropes. I just could not make out how *Cizara* had grown a second storey!

8
The off-season

Back from the expedition I had to admit to a feeling of relief. *Cizara* was still afloat, and had beaten the Crinan closure, and I had survived the over-rapid motor journey home. Another 'off-season' was about to commence, the winter months when monster-hunting was impractical, and when new ideas would germinate. There would be talks and lectures to give and the usual spider's web of human interest. Soon, four invitations to speak at universities arrived. The first, in October, from the Biological Society of London's Queen Mary College. I had spoken there twice before, and was friendly with the technical staff, who always treated the subject fairly.

The universities of East Anglia, Liverpool and Wales fixed dates; the latter for a talk at the Marine Science Laboratories on the island of Anglesey, across the Menai Straits. The publication of Birmingham University's sonar results, obtained in August 1968 in Urquhart Bay by Professor D. Gordon Tucker and Hugh Braithwaite, a senior research assistant, had caused a great deal of interest; and on Christmas Eve there was another surprise – a letter from my publishers to commission *Project Water Horse* as an unexpected new book in the series.

In early January 1969 I had lunch with David James in London. It was eight years since we first met and it was interesting to discuss the progress the LNI (as it was now more conveniently referred to) had made since then. Characteristically, it was an American who had helped the most. Professor Roy Mackal of Chicago University had worked like a beaver to gain support, once he had visited Loch Ness and satisfied himself about the Monster evidence. Full of energy and enthusiasm, it was largely due to his efforts that Field Enterprises Educational Corporation donated research funds to the LNI in 1967, continuing in support until the season's end in 1970.

After lunch, we went to the Boat Show, at Earls Court to meet Tom Lack on the Bobcat Stand. There was a Mark 2 8-metre catamaran on display, with better accommodation, and the new 10-metre boat. I looked over it with a practical eye. It was, in my opinion, the best boat in the show, and I marked it down for future expeditions; little realizing that four years later it would be the first catamaran ever to go round Cape Horn, with the amazing Swale family aboard. Later that evening I met two Americans who were concerned with underwater research, and went with them to the restaurant above Victoria Station, where the LNI's membership held their annual Christmas party. It was informal, with a buffet supper following a slide and film show, which brought the subject up to date. We discussed Birmingham's sonar results, which were explained to us by a member of the scientific team. The electronic display was not easy to interpret, but its significance was hard to doubt.

It was an interesting day, and a productive one, because I was told the LNI might sponsor me if I could re-charter a catamaran and put it back on the water for three months – and undertake certain experiments for them, such as dredging for skeletal remains. It was feasible, so I tried again to obtain *Cizara*, but with negative results. It was a disappointment, but I could not blame the Smiths who much enjoyed their summer sailing. It just didn't fit in.

There were alternatives – and I felt hopeful about them, because in 1969 I would have the backing of money and experience. I could either charter another catamaran, and sail it up, or perhaps make a down payment on a new boat and embark on the round trip originally planned.

After speaking at East Anglia University in late January, I travelled up to the Menai Straits and over Telford's historic suspension bridge, calling to mind 'Telford's Weir' at Loch Ness – and so to the Marine Science Laboratories, where specimen dogfish swam about in tanks, awaiting experiment.

I was shown round, then entertained to dinner, and it was during this meal that I found out about another odd coincidence. There were, I suppose, half a dozen of us sitting round the table, drawn together by chance, and yet the scientist opposite me, from the

Department of Physical Oceanography, had been working aboard the *Prince Maddog* research vessel when she entered Loch Ness. It was their work vessel. I inquired whether it would go back in 1969, because there might be a chance of using it, or getting the department to do some work for the LNI. I was told it was unlikely, but not impossible.

The lecture proved a success, with perhaps 300 people in the audience, and I was glad of the opportunity to talk to marine scientists for a change.

With time to build a new catamaran running out, I phoned Tom Lack to see if he could suggest another charter, or the purchase of a second-hand boat. I inquired about the boat in Loch Ryan, but she was not available until mid-September. This was too late because of the risk of autumn gales. It was a pity – but the catamaran expedition had taught me four lessons:
1 that having mastered a big boat single-handed I need no longer be afraid of the water at Loch Ness;
2 that in anything but flat calm conditions it was better to mount cameras ashore, due to the movement of the boat, even with the stability resulting from a multi-hull design;
3 that the surface environment was best for concentrated watching – because it imparted a sense of closeness: of invading the Monster's domain. This awakened the alert instincts of the hunter;
4 that the big catamaran was a good platform but that a smaller boat could be used if it was stabilized somehow by outriggers.

Another alternative would be to stalk the Monster from the air. The idea had occurred to me during the hunt in 1968, and although noise would be a problem, and the lack of forced landing places a hazard, I had wondered whether to hire a small aeroplane, and climb to 5,000 ft at one end of the loch, then glide the length of it with engine throttled back, ready to dive in on the Beast and shoot film if it appeared on the surface.

Later in January I rang up a friend on the staff of *Flight* magazine – Neil Harrison, the assistant editor, and I put the case to him. He suggested a powered glider, because it would have the advantage of almost silent flight – maintaining height on just a whiff of throttle, and could operate out of Inverness airport nearby. He told me that a new design of tandem powered glider was being built in Germany, and that he would try and arrange to borrow it, and use it at Loch Ness as a part of the demonstration tour. He would act as pilot, which would give me a chance to work the cameras properly. I was delighted by this, and promptly opened a file entitled 'Operation Albatross'. Before I could do anything practical about it however, there was an unexpected hold-up, caused by the need to have a piece of metal extricated from between the fourth and fifth metacarpal bones of my right hand, where it had remained embedded for twenty-eight years. In 1941, when serving with the Home Guard, the 'Dad's Army' of legend, I had been accidentally shot by another young man, who was to be killed himself in a live ammunition exercise shortly afterwards. The Home Guard in those days was, in fact, a serious business, and in all forms of military training accidents occur, for which no one can be blamed.

In April I drove to an orthopaedic hospital and was admitted through the laborious process of the National Health Service. I was then ordered to bathe, wash my hair, and submit to the shaving of my whole forearm. By now I began to wonder whether things had got muddled up and I was in for an amputation.

I was wheeled into the operating theatre, and given a local anaesthetic which killed the pain, but left my hand sensitive to the smallest stimulus – the blood trickling down following the incision, and the nauseating probing that followed. I could feel the instruments grating against bone. I began to drift off into a natural oblivion, only to be aroused by a cheerful lady anaesthetist who twirled a handle, tipping my head down at an acute angle. We carried on a somewhat stilted conversation.

I drove home that afternoon and a week later, when the bandages came off, I found a puffed-up boxing glove of a hand, the wound clamped by jet-black stitching which crawled across it like a tropical centipede. The injury appalled me, but such is the power of the body to heal itself that within two or three weeks the swelling subsided, and my fingers regained their strength and some of their sensitivity.

This small operation delayed the next phase of 'Project Water Horse' by approximately a month. Developments in the powered glider project also went badly, and although Neil Harrison made arrangements to test the new German tandem machine, they came to nothing.

We had agreed to meet before driving out to a flying show and exhibition at Biggin Hill, the air station which won immortal fame during the Battle of Britain, but when we got there, we could not find the machine or the pilot, and learned through traffic control that neither had arrived from Europe.

Neil continued his inquiries, however, and was later able to arrange a flight in a different type of machine at Booker airfield, no more than an hour's drive away from my home. It had side by side seating, and an engine which produced barely 30 horse-power. I guessed it must be the lowest-powered two-seater in existence, but felt the risk worth taking, and travelled over one Sunday morning.

Standing on the grass aerodrome with small planes taking off and buzzing round reminded me of my time in the RAF, and at De Havilland, during the War, when my whole life was taken up with flight, and the means of engineering it. It was a warm day, but a thunderstorm was building up. I met the pilot, and he showed me the glider, which was an unusual shoulder-wing type. I peered at the engine – a tiny flat four, then walked round the machine.

On the tail fin, I saw something which had an odd effect on me. A single word, painted on, indicating no doubt the place of manufacture – innocent enough, and yet it was a word with connotations of disaster, which pierced my confidence like a dagger thrust of ice – Dachau.

Clambering into the machine, I closed my eyes to the gathering storm, and as we taxied, rumbling across the grass, on a tiny two-wheeled undercarriage, raindrops began to patter on the fabric.

We took off, and flew in the gathering gloom, buffeted by turbulence. There was no elbow room in the cockpit. I made an attempt to shoot film through a small round hole in the canopy, but it was impossible – and I realized that without modifications to it I could not use the camera.

Returning, the pilot lost height before shutting the engine down for a glide approach, the wind whistling over the airframe. We crossed two-thirds of the airfield before spoilers brought us down to go skidding across the grass.

It was an expert landing, and I scrambled out, to spend the next half hour sheltering under the wing in torrents of rain, before pushing the glider back into the hangar.

Later, saying goodbye to Neil Harrison, I thanked him for his help but said that I must shelve 'Operation Albatross'. I returned home, and told my wife – who looked relieved. The idea was still a good one in principle, if a powered glider with tandem seating and a bubble canopy could be obtained – but we had been unable to arrange it.

Reverting once more to the question of boats, I had to decide on the best type of hull to use on the water, and again sought the help of Jim Ewing, the indefatigable Scot. We looked at several craft, one of which was a 15 ft cruiser, but it was too light and there was not enough freeboard. It was a toy boat and could easily have sunk in rough water on the Ness.

A third craft, however, a Micro Plus 500 appealed to both of us. She was elegantly shaped and moulded in fibreglass. There was a small cabin, with shelves and a cupboard inside: four shatterproof glass windows, a roof-hatch, and a big cockpit aft, with a double reinforced transom, and good freeboard. Previously two 40 horsepower outboards had driven her at 50 m.p.h., but with a small 9·2 Chrysler engine fitted, speed would be far less than that – perhaps eight or ten knots at the most. It would be fast enough however, and ensure economy.

More importantly, considering the good points and the bad (a sixteen-footer still seemed too small for me) and the economics, we decided in favour of it.

Within a few days we put the hull on the water, slipped easily from the trailer, and tested it with both engines: the Chrysler, which performed as expected, and the little three-horse Johnson, which went with my inflatable dinghy. It proved a useful spare, and could move the boat at two or three knots. After my experience with *Cizara* I was determined to have a stand-by engine, which I could install quickly.

Towing *Water Horse* home, I parked her in the driveway, where she at once became of interest to our children, who climbed into the cockpit. Soon they were off on imaginary voyages, throwing out the anchor at intervals, and dodging ferocious attacks by sharks which were obviously of the man-eating variety. I could see the little craft had already begun her adventures, but before work could begin at Loch Ness I needed to fit stabilizers. The hull was only 5 ft 6 in. in the beam, and as such was useless as a camera platform.

I thought of using floats on outriggers, but in rough water these would not be of much help. The boat would continue to rock about. Jim Ewing suggested two old dustbin lids, as an alternative! The idea was not as crazy as it sounded because water is a heavy fluid, and with two lids working in opposition on either side below the surface the boat could hardly wobble. The lids would act as powerful hydraulic dampers.

Using two halves of the frame from a children's swing which had been rusting in the garden, and various pieces of timber, I constructed a pair of outrigger arms and braced them to the cockpit.

It was a contraption, but as an engineer, I knew my work on Loch Ness could depend on its ability to stabilize the boat; and under the surface the dustbin lids would not appear ridiculous. They would probably be mistaken for sonar reflectors – and as it turned out, that is what happened. More than one journalist in his eagerness to write sensationally described my equipment as 'including sonar'; which of course was nonsense.

The last and most tedious job was to build a towing frame for the Jaguar, by now twelve years old and outside the ready spares category. I needed something strong enough to mount a winch, in addition to the trailer for the boat.

The solution lay in a welded framework, which bolted through the chassis. It was a fiddling job, made more difficult by my injured hand, but on 29 June 1969 I left home early in the morning, with all the equipment stowed and in working order. I was approximately one month late, but the delay meant I would not have to spend quite so long away from my family. I would miss them, and I did not enjoy saying goodbye at all.

9
Summer, submarines and sonar

Aboard *Water Horse*
Urquhart Bay
Loch Ness
July 15th 1969

Dear Everybody,

This is the first of the letters I will write to keep you up to date with what's going on.

After leaving you all early that Sunday morning, I motored northwards, feeling a little sad, but in compensation the trip through the country lanes of Northamptonshire was lovely. The boat trailed easily, though it did not take to rough roads, giving one the impression it was connected to the car with a thick strand of elastic. I think it may have been the bumper bending, but as I could not actually watch it, I ignored it, and periodic checks showed everything to be in order.

I arrived at Peter's in mid-afternoon, having covered 330 miles, which says a lot for an early start. They were all in fine trim at the farm. I spent a welcome day with them, then left on July 1st, crossing the great suspension bridge over the Firth of Forth, and so northwards, to Inverness.

I drove on to the Caledonian Ship Canal office at Clachnaharry to make my number with the manager there, and from him I learned of the excitement going on at the Ness, with the two submarines at Urquhart Bay, one belonging to Vickers, a sophisticated research vehicle called *Pisces* and Dan Taylor's little one-man job *Viperfish* which had yet to be launched.

On to Fort Augustus, in brilliant sunlight, I passed the spot near Cherry Island (where you got your sighting last year) and examined the launching ramp. It was in need of repair, but I reckoned I could just manage to slip *Water Horse* there. Had it not been suitable it would have meant going back forty miles to the Muirtown three-ton crane, and lifting the boat into the canal, and so into the Ness.

Having done some shopping in F.A., I went back and started preparations, only to find the job impossible on my own. It proved far more difficult than I had expected, to jack-knife the car and boat into position, and with so much at stake I couldn't risk an early disaster. I phoned the expedition, and asked for a crew to help, but as it was such a fine day most were off on camera duty, so I was told it might take an hour or two to round them up. I set to work stripping the car and boat of gear, ready for the launch. Perhaps an hour later the proprietor of the hotel, nearby, came down and offered to help. It was a tricky operation, but we got *Water Horse* into the loch safely.

I spent the night tied up alongside, surrounded by the chaos of equipment, and the next day, which was wet, tried to sort things out. I just could not see how to move in such a microscopic space – compared with *Cizara* – which is a floating hotel by comparison. Late that evening, I set off for the tie-up point up the river Tarff, promised me by the monks, but it was dismally cold and wet, and approaching the river mouth *Water Horse* went hard aground on what appeared to be a ridge of stones blocking the channel. That gave me another jolt, and for a ghastly moment I stood waiting to see the loch water pouring in. I managed to pole off with an oar, and went back to the little bay, and spent the next four days and nights there, anchored, away from the pier with its clatter of youngsters and fishermen leaping in and out of boats.

It was a lonely time, and a damp one, and I struggled to keep some sort of order aboard. Obviously the expedition was going to tax my patience. Every move I made had to be a conscious one if I was not to bang my head or sit on a camera or some other vital piece of equipment. But it wasn't all bad. The cooker was a success, my bunk was O.K., and the visibility marvellous from inside the boat. Once I got the gear into corners and nooks, stuffed up the bow and under the seats, and remembered where the hell I had put it – I could begin to move about. I decided too, to go through the boat with an eagle eye, and transfer all non-vital equipment back to the Jaguar.

By Sunday, I was beginning to see daylight, and had found that the 'dustbin damping' outriggers were a stunning success. They damped the small-boat wobble to a degree that made a camera platform comparable with *Cizara*.

I left Inchnacardoch on Monday, a week after getting to the Ness, and set course for Urquhart Bay, having parked the car at the Abbey – confidently expecting to return within a day or two, once the sub. was launched. About a mile from the starting point, with a strong wind, the engine faded out and *Water Horse* began to buck uncontrollably. I realized that small boats don't behave like big catamarans and hurriedly tried to start the engine again, fearing the worst.

It started at once, to my surprise, and buzzed away contentedly for the remainder of the journey, at full throttle, pushing along at about 8 knots. I think it must have been a spot of water in the petrol condensing off the tank.

Opposite Invermoriston the wind increased, and in no time we were in rough water. I kicked the driver's seat down, and stood at the wheel with legs braced. We surged forward and as the wind increased I noticed that *Water Horse* was putting her nose down and surfing! It was an exhilarating ride, and so lonely, with nothing but the rock-walls towering above on either side. The sun glinted off the wake and the pursuing waves, and I made a foolish attempt to catch it on film, letting go of the wheel. The boat immediately broached, and for a moment I thought she would roll over. It gave me a fright. Four or five miles further on the wind abated and rain began to deluge in icy sheets which swept across the water. I put on my 'oilies' and stood with my back to it comfortably enough, and in time it stopped, leaving only an inky surface with the swell coursing through it.

Perhaps an hour later we rounded Castle Urquhart, entering the bay in sunlight. It was sheltered and calm, and I tied up at the small floating LNI (Loch Ness Investigation) jetty, close to Temple Pier. There was a great deal of activity, with a film company occupying the shore, building a gigantic model monster, for use in a new

Sherlock Holmes film; and next to it the bright orange submarine *Pisces*, with its attendant score of technicians. I was told they expected to use it to propel the Model Monster, once they got it in the water.

I was also told that, due to a technical snag, Dan Taylor's little one-man sub. would not be launched until next day, so the throng of sightseers would be disappointed, not to mention the press photographers. I went ashore to visit Urquhart Lodge, or rather the garage behind it in which the submarine was parked. It was an odd sight. A tiny yellow cigar, made out of fibreglass – hundreds of layers of it, with all sorts of external cables and equipment and a conning tower with thick observation portholes. It may have been a do-it-yourself job, but one got the impression the owner knew what he was about. I met Dan briefly, and liked him – a quiet southerner. Equipment was everywhere. . . .

I spent the night tied up at the pier comfortably enough, except for the thumping noise generated by wavelets as they collided with the hard chine of the hull.

The next day brought the press back in droves, with frogmen, and local boatmen and hundreds of onlookers and cars causing a traffic jam above. Fortunately the sun came out, and a further launching delay of 24 hours did not upset anyone.

The day after that caused a disturbance which must have been unique to this part of the Highlands. Dan Taylor's sub. was towed down from Drumnadrochit on its curious three-wheeled trailer, and hoisted up by the crane used for lifting *Pisces* in and out of the water. The shore at Temple Pier, which is privately owned, was seething with pressmen, the film company employees, the LNI volunteers, and the tourist multitudes above. On the water frogmen darted about blowing spouts of water out of their schnorkels, and on the surface boats jockeyed for position. It was a form of three-ringed circus, but when the little submarine refused to submerge because of ballast problems it was decided to postpone the operation until these were properly sorted out.

For the next week I moved about the bay, driven from one spot to another by the ever-changing wind and the small boat's need for protection. I seemed to be constantly up-anchoring, and with the light remaining until after midnight, and dawn at 4 a.m., due to the northerly latitude, sleep became a dreamed-of luxury.

Letter the second

Aboard *Water Horse*
Urquhart Bay
August 12th 1969

Perhaps I should say half-time letter, because I've been on the water six weeks already, and the days and weeks slip by in such an extraordinary way I often forget what day it is. I was once three days out, and I'm sure the local shopkeeper who put me right thought I was barmy: I said 'Is it Wednesday or Thursday?' when it was Saturday afternoon!

This may give you some idea of the dreamy surroundings in which I have come to live, because after the early mistakes I settled down to a quiet routine which might best be described by the phrase 'Where'er the wind bloweth – that's where I goeth'.

At the moment I'm anchored up the delta end of the bay, and the wind bloweth – or is beginning to, and as typing with the boat going up and down is difficult, I'll have to move, using the electric outboard which moves me with stabilisers down in silence, at about one mile an hour. . . . Ah, that's better. We are now almost in among the reed beds. It is a lonely and lovely part of the bay with, curiously enough, a shelving approach of sea sand infiltrated with river silt. Shades of the past, and not so long distant either, when the Ness was an arm of the sea. As you may remember from the literature, the Beast has been reported out of water here too, though I know of no recent accounts. It could certainly get out here easily enough, and I watch the shoreline for signs of it.

To go back to where I left off – very briefly, I came to terms with my situation about the second week in July, when I visited the Carys' high up on the west shore of the bay. They have an old converted croft house, and several acres of steep hillside leading down to the water in the vicinity of Urquhart Castle. They are the retired folk of 'boundless hospitality' to whom I referred in *The*

Leviathans; and they haven't changed a bit. Basil soon suggested putting down a mooring for *Water Horse* close under the lee of the shore at a spot called Goat Rock, and with the prevailing westerlies I hastily agreed, because it meant I would get some proper sleep. It was away from the constant activity and chatter of the pier across the bay.

Within a day or two a routine developed, which I have followed ever since. I get up with the light –photographic light that is, which now starts at about six, set up the gear on the big tripod, which is strapped down to the hull, and watch in absolute quietness until about nine. I tidy ship, which is difficult in such a confined space, then slip moorings, and allow the wind ripple to take me hither or yon. Sometimes I drift out into deep water in the loch proper, and sometimes just potter about in the bay – then about an hour later on most mornings a wind gets up – I call it the 'ten o'clock wind'; with stability lost I motor over to the LNI pier and exchange pleasantries with the overnight camera crew, who have kept an eye on Dan's little sub. which sits on its three-wheeled cradle just clear of the water. The cradle is winched up and down a shelf of stones and the submarine floated off for diving operations.

Of course the ten o'clock wind isn't always on time, and when this happens I continue the drift until it does appear, except in 'Nessie Weather' – the hot flat calm we all hope for, when I drift about for most of the day.

In the early part of the hunt, *Pisces* was diving a great deal, and making almost daily discoveries. Huge potholes and fissures in the bottom of the loch, confounding the echo search equipment from the surface which had plotted a flat, almost featureless plain of silt. They shot film of it, and discovered too an old wreck of a ship off Temple Pier; some guns or muskets which they could not quite pick up with their grab – and two places of great depth, beyond the previously accepted maximum, which had stood at 754 feet off the castle, since the loch was first mapped underwater. The echo-sounder's new depth of 820 feet and then an abyssal 975 feet near the first Cobb marker post: the place where *Crusader* started her ill-fated record-breaking run in 1952. They had two other experiences of note, as you must have heard by now: the big blip on the sonar

Plate 1 Driftsailing alone on the big cat. was a marvellous
experience.

Plate 2 (above) Anchored in Urquhart Bay.
Plate 3 (above right) *Cizara*.
Plate 4 (right) *Water Horse* with the *Moo-scow* alongside, drifting past Urquhart Castle.

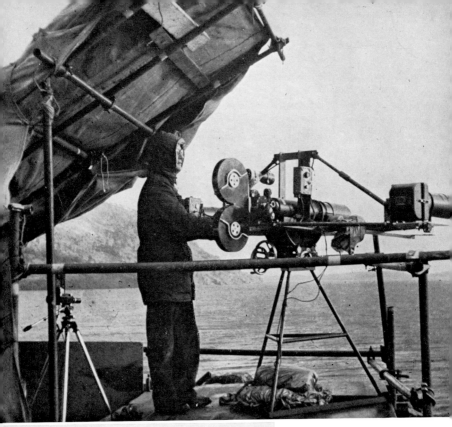

Plate 5 (above) The 'Big Rig' at the castle battlements site; David James's expedition in 1964.

Plate 6 (left) Bearded John Addey lent a hand on the second 'Island' expedition.

Plate 7 (above)
Simplified equipment at
the LNI's main site,
Achnahannet; 1965-1972.
Plate 8 (right) Mobile
camera vehicle on station
opposite Foyers.

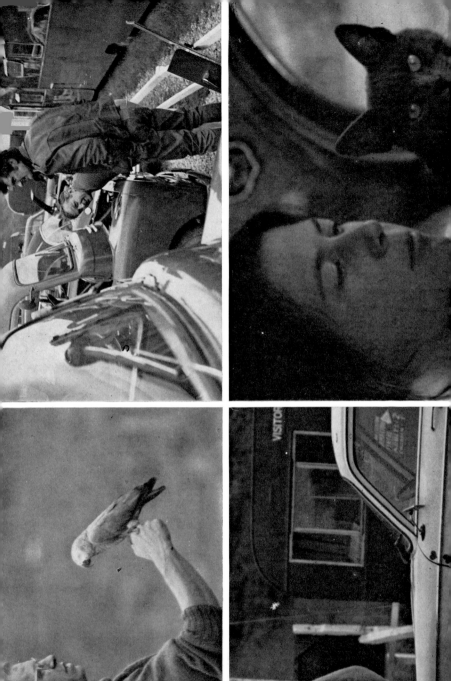

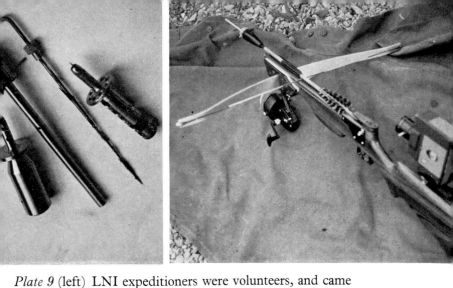

Plate 9 (left) LNI expeditioners were volunteers, and came from many different places. Personalities and pets varied too— (top) 'Rip' and 'Mac' the parrot; 'Matey' (upright); Eric; Holly and 'Mu' the cat, represented England, Africa, Australia, France, America and Persia respectively.

Plate 10 (above left) My three designs of 'coring head', showing skewer arrangement, developed 1962-66.

Plate 11 (above right) The cross-bow increased the range of the tissue-sampling dart, but proved too slow and complicated. I stopped using it in 1971.

Plate 12 (below) In 1969 a film company built a model Monster with animated head and neck. Unfortunately, it sank.

Plate 13 In 1969 *Pisces*, the Vickers submersible, spent many hours underwater exploring Loch Ness, and found it to be deeper than expected— just under 1,000 ft as registered on sonar.

Plate 14 *Viperfish*, Dan Taylor's little one-man fibreglass sub. worked in Urquhart Bay, but had a limited performance. *Water Horse* was in support.

Plate 15 Wing-commander Kenneth Wallis, C. Eng., A.F.R.Ae.S, (at left) designs and builds his own one-man autogyros—

Plate 16—and flies them too with great skill and enthusiasm. Below is *Rangitea*, Bob Love's sonar boat, and Ivor Newby's *Kelpie* (right).

Plate 17 (above) The irrepressible 'Academy' team from the USA (left to right, Carol and Bob Rines, Dr Charles Wyckoff, Bob Needleman and a young helper) lower the automatic sonar-trigger camera rig to the bottom in Urquhart Bay, below *Smuggler*, Wing-commander Cary's famous yacht.
Plate 18 (below) Sonar in *Water Horse*. Dr. Martin Klein.

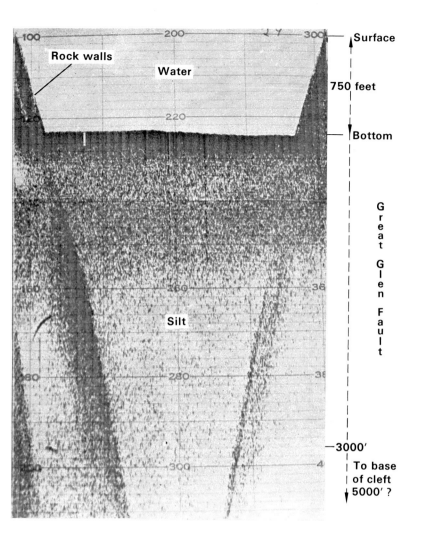

Rock walls

Water

Surface

750 feet

Bottom

Great Glen Fault

Silt

−3000′

To base
of cleft
5000′ ?

Plate 19 Raytheon sonar chart recording made from
Water Horse in July 1974 by Dr Robert H. Rines appears
to show the continuing line of rock-walls beneath the
bottom silt of Loch Ness. A discovery of unique
geological interest.

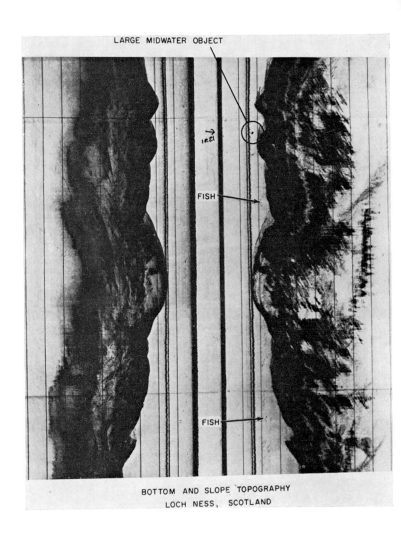

Plate 20 'Blip' off the Horse Shoe. Sidescan Sonar, 1970.

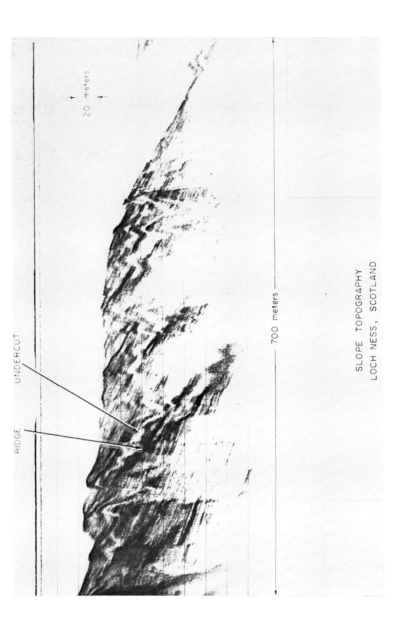

Plate 21 Marty Klein's proof of the underwater caverns.

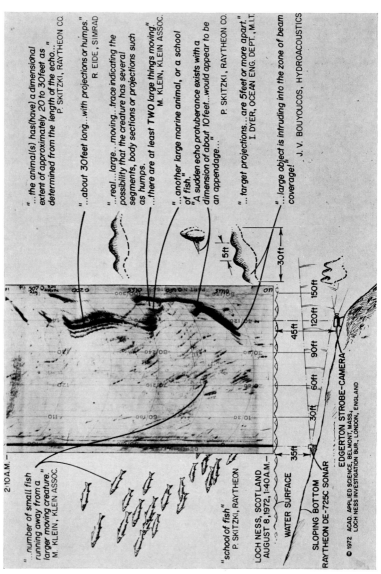

Plate 22 (above) 1972 sonar chart, recording a bull's-eye.
Plate 23 (right) The Rines/Edgerton underwater 'flipper' picture obtained in 1972, some 45 ft down in Urquhart Bay. It shows a huge paddle-like structure 6-8 ft long and 2-3 ft broad. Coincidentally, a sonar chart recording machine indicated passage of an underwater object 20-30 ft in length. The picture was obtained using a synchronous strobe-flash camera, prepared by Professor Harold Edgerton at MIT, and has been computer-enhanced. See Appendix A.

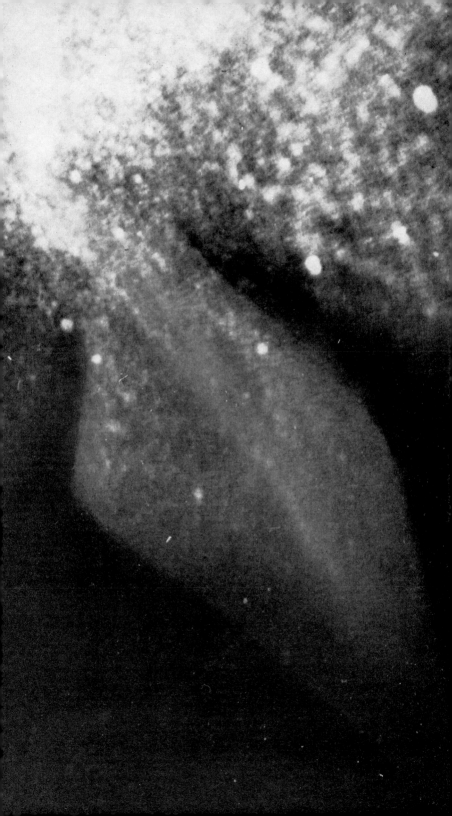

Plate 24 Hunter on Urquhart Bay. In 1972 and 1973 I lived aboard for five months while probing Lochs Ness and Morar.

screen, about 40 feet in length, by interpretation, which shoved off
when they approached it, and a strange vortex which spun them
round in a big hole far down near the bottom. The submarine
weighed eleven tons, but was swirled around, and had to blow tanks
to get out of it. I think it frightened them, because it could have
been caused by a current, or vortex, or possibly a sink hole in the
bottom of the loch with the water running out of it. If the latter,
they might have ended up sucked into it like a bath plug – for keeps.
Being a fault zone, the whole length of the Great Glen could be
seamed with cracks and fissures underwater, as it is above.

Another diversion was caused by the film company and their
monolithic model monster, for use in the Sherlock Holmes picture
(though how it has found a way into the Holmes' saga defeats me).
They spent a lot of time and money towing it about, and making
artificial mist to film it through. The bay was alive with boats for a
while, and the constant disturbance of engines, which of course put
an end to monster-hunting . . . the real kind that is. But it was
fascinating to watch.

The model was about 30 feet in length and weighed four or five
tons. It had three huge humps and a long neck with a ferocious head,
and bulging eyes. It could move its head about and open its mouth,
and the eyes lit up too. I believe the whole contraption cost about
£10,000. I was lucky to film it from the western hillside one day
when they started tests. A cable was secured to it from the shore,
then a power winch dragged the 'Beastie' through the water at quite
a speed, which, with the vane beneath, produced a diving effect –
the head and neck moving the while.

I saw this, and having the Bolex camera with me, flung myself
down and, resting the lens on the carrying case, shot off some film.
I then slithered down to the shore, and shot some more film in
close-up as the model went by. It gave me quite an eerie feeling. To
finish up, a boat appeared with frogmen, who got on to the model,
then in through a small trap-door in its back, rounding off the
sequence.

The very next day the great model monster plunged to the bottom
of the loch in rough water, and was lost – or, as a local newspaper
put it, 'went to join its ain folk'.

G

Continued 15th August which is, I feel sure, a Friday – or is it? But no matter, I am out on the deep water in perfect calm, with mist veiling the far mountains of the south shore. It is fantastically beautiful, with a sort of cascade of sunlight streaming down through it and gleaming off the water. The castle is to starboard. Wee *Water Horse* now looks odd, draped in camouflaged sheeting, cut up from the shrouds around *Cizara*, but it is effective, and blends with the shoreline. Indeed, the other day nature paid us a compliment. A flight of wild duck nearly flew into us – and for weeks now I have been watching and filming a family of Great Crested Grebes, diving birds, nearby. They were chicks when I got here, but now are twice the size, and they cover great distances each day, thinking nothing of swimming across the bay and back, a distance of a mile and a half at least. They are pretty things with pointed beaks, and a ruff of feathers to the side of the head. They can also *run* on the water. Honestly, exactly that, and very quickly too, for perhaps a hundred yards at a stretch. They are still too young to fly, and I have tried to film them in slow motion doing this, leaving V-wakes like a small flotilla of speed boats. They absolutely pelt along, then dive as a final resort. I don't like to frighten them, so veer off before they run out of breath. . . .

But back to the model monster, and the many other things of note. The film I shot came out well, in fact it must be unique, and it may be invaluable in providing a direct contrast between the most expensive model-Nessie ever built, and, perhaps, the real thing; but we must wait and see.

Altogether I've shot about 1,000 feet of film as backing – and nearly all of it appears to be good, with colours well in balance; which is an encouragement. It has given me some priceless scenic effects.

But it is not all dreamery. In fact I shall remember this expedition for the great variety of human contacts. The LNI fields a team of about 20–25 people each fortnight, and their camera crews change stations every now and then, and when I go to the pier I meet them, or rather two or three who guard the camera there, and the sub. It is nice to get ashore periodically, and talk to folk, and inevitably there is much fun and good humour. I get water there too, and am able to arrange a swop of batteries for the electric outboard. Dan Taylor is, of course, constantly charging batteries for the sub.

Viperfish, by the way, is now operating and it dives to the bottom in the bay. Dan was down the other afternoon, and had a big trout swimming round the portholes in his conning tower looking *in*. He has lights which help a bit, but the water is so inklike even *Pisces* with her terrific lights can only see a few yards at best. Underwater, sonar is the tool to use, and we waited upon the arrival of Bob Love, the American underwater search expert with his box of tricks; and the Birmingham University team, and Plessey's waterborne equipment to be mounted in *Jessie Ellen*. All this seems to be scheduled for September. Meanwhile Dan is working up his boat, and doing everything sensibly and quietly. He is level-headed, and in my view has a lot of courage. The press seem to have got bored, and do not bother him nearly as much. In fact, the pier end of the bay is now relatively quiet, with *Pisces* away tomorrow to start diving in Loch Linnhe, which is salt water. She and her crew will be missed, I'm sure, particularly Bob Eastaugh her skipper, who is a big strapping fellow. The sub-mariners are a breed of men apart, and I admire them, but for some reason the underwater search does not draw me like photography.

The ten o'clock wind is here (about an hour late) and I'm drifting down towards the Cobb mile post again. It is a lonely spot – perhaps harbouring the shadows of disaster. I think I'll move away. . . . Ivor and Christine in their big glass powerboat, with Ron, another monster-hunting independent aboard, have just tied up alongside for coffee. I'm not bothering with surnames, because no one seems to use them and it is quite impossible to remember them all – anyway, they moved into the bay about a week ago, and are doing much the same as I, but without all the falderal of equipment. It's nice to have some waterborne company, and we often tie up alongside and drift. His tiny dinghy, a sort of li-lo affair which we call the 'Banana boat' is even more easy to fall out of than the *Moo-scow*, which is the name I have given the inflatable dinghy which trails around after me. It reminds me of a large and rather dim but friendly animal which wants desperately to please, but sometimes does the opposite. Sometimes, I'd swear the thing was alive. It casts itself off and drifts away, and when I go after it, the moment I try and catch it with my boat-hook, the breeze freshens and it eludes me. It's quite a jolly old thing really and is indispensable for getting ashore, and as a safety boat – or life raft.

10
Autumn leaves and hurricanes

Letter the last

Aboard *Water Horse*
Urquhart Bay
Thursday, Sept. 11th, 1969

I'm sitting in 'me cabin', looking out across the bay through the glass windows – having just cooked a very pleasing lunch of lamb chops and peas, swilled down with Pepsi-Cola!

There is a strange collection of boats around the LNI floating pier, set off by the backdrop of the far shore, the castle, the rough water, the towering south shore mountains and the grey leaden sky. It is cold, but the rain has stopped, thank goodness. My worst enemy in this very little boat.

Perhaps a hundred yards away there is an old rowing boat: black clinker-built hull, with a green paint strip round the top. A man is standing up, fly fishing. He is old too, with white hair, and his body marvellously upright compensates for the pitch and roll of his craft. The fly rod bends in a gentle arc to the movement of his hand.

Astern, Ivor Newby's gleaming white cruiser trails the 'Banana boat' which has a nosey look about it – a longish snout, which twitches up and down with the movement of the water; and two rubber-patch eyes set too close together. For some time now we've noticed the 'Banana boat' making up to *Moo-scow*, and when hitched up together he jostles her. The *Moo-scow* is more than twice his size, and pays no attention whatsoever – or could it be her mental faculties aren't up to it; that she doesn't even notice the intrusion? Experience tells me this is probably the case. . . .

On Temple Pier nearby, where the Great Model Monster sat, the sonar teams from Birmingham University, and Plessey and the

Navy are preparing their equipment, with ITN and the *Daily Mail* in attendance. I don't know what results they'll get, but one thing is certain, the hunt is almost up for me, and on Sunday week I will move out of this bay which has provided shelter, and so much else besides during the past three months. But it is not over yet, and in order to provide some continuity I must tell you a little of what has taken place since I wrote the half-time letter.

During the latter part of August the hunt was galvanized by the arrival of the Petersons. Ken, the Producer for Walt Disney Productions, with whom I had exchanged correspondence, and Harriet, his wife. He came here with the object of shooting colour for a short TV film, and I'm sure he and his expert Scottish camera team have made a brilliant job of it.

The LNI crews and just about everyone concerned this summer became involved in the fascinating game of film making, with the loch providing the best variety of moods and colour as a backdrop.

I think the Petersons enjoyed their fortnight very much, and went home with some unique film, covering all aspects of the chase: the witnesses, scenery, songs and entertainments at the 'Lodge', the meeting ground for monster-hunters in Glen Urquhart.

The Lodge, by the way, provides a spontaneous form of entertainment once or twice a week, known as a 'kaly' (spelled 'ceilidh', in Gaelic), at which kilts are worn, the pipes are played, and where individuals sing and dance into the early hours, prompted by a dram or two of that Scottish stimulus known to some as the 'water of life'.

Looking back to my jotted notes for other points of interest, I see that on August 17th, Ivor Newby 'falls overboard for the 4th time, clutching anchor'. Falling in is more easy to understand when one stands on a fibreglass boat, which gets ice-slippery when wet. Were it not for my camouflage sheeting on *Water Horse*, I'd have been in myself several times already.

The night following this incident, Ivor felt a sudden bump when his boat was at anchor, and shining his flash-light out of the window thought he saw the 'Banana boat' drifting off. Looking round however, to his surprise, he found it was in fact still tied up astern! By now, the other object had disappeared, and he wonders in consequence whether it could have been the Monster, swimming into the anchor cable underneath the boat, before surfacing nearby. I think it is possible, because he anchors in fifteen to twenty feet of water. I always back up for the night as shallow as I dare before hooking up (there is an art in doing this properly), but in shallow water one is just that much nearer the rocks, and if the wind changes a bad situation can develop.

Waking up to cast off in the pitch black night in rough water and pouring rain is not my idea of fun – nor is the journey across the bay in search of shelter. I've had to do this several times, with no more than a single glint of light a mile away far up on the mountainside to act as a beacon. It's lonely, and wet and dangerous and one longs to get back into one's bunk, and forget about boats and weather – but then the calm water welcomes you, and pretty soon the sun comes up again. Another day. Experience is the key to boating on the Ness – and what I call the 'belt and braces' technique. Never should you rely on one 'string' only – the term we amateurs have given to all ropes, sheets, cordage, lines and cables, regardless of type or thickness. It's all 'string' to us, though we do admit to 'best string' sometimes, or 'my longest string'. We've even got the professionals calling it string in some cases, which makes it a lot easier.

On August 26th I went down-loch and aboard *Prince Maddog*, the big research vessel, which I first spotted from *Cizara* last year. Isn't it odd that *on the same day* that I logged the appearance of this strange vessel in the Ness (the 19th September 1968) the secretary of the 'Endeavour Society' of the University College of North Wales should write inviting me to lecture, and that when I got there I found they owned the vessel, and had dinner with its chief scientific officer who had been aboard at the time. As I went alongside in *Water Horse* this summer the same Dr Simpson invited me on board to take a look around.

The ship was anchored in 600 feet of water, and was involved in deep thermocline testing. It was, of course, packed with electronic gear, and had six scientists aboard as well as a crew of eight. She was in the 300-ton class, and while we were on deck a most curious trick of light occurred, which I tried to record on film. Somehow, the surface ripple was reflecting sunlight like the carrier wave of a radio beacon. It produced a unique effect, with waves of light flashing towards and past us at perhaps a thousand miles an hour – or appearing to. I have never seen anything quite like it.

We had supper aboard, served by a steward wearing a spotless white jacket. It transported me back over the years to my youth, and China, and meals served aboard coastal steamers. The thrumm of engines in the background, and the unmistakable odours of a ship remain unalterable.

It made a pleasant interlude, and on the next day Ivor's boat and mine, the yellow submarine and the LNI's lifeboat all became involved in a film sequence shot from the air by a helicopter, in the middle of the loch, opposite the castle.

It was great fun, and a bit of a circus stunt, with the downdraught from the 'copter kicking up the spray and the roar from its engines attracting throngs of tourists, who stopped their cars to watch. The submarine dived and resurfaced, with the boats whirling round it, then spinning off like sparks from a catherine wheel. In the middle of this I ran out of fuel but managed to tank up again without spilling too much. Petrol mixed with oil is slippery stuff, most undesirable in the cockpit; and there is always the risk of fire. The next day our boats had moved some fifteen miles down-loch to Invermoriston, with Ken Peterson and his camera-men aboard to shoot background film. They returned by road, so Ivor and I decided to anchor there for the night, because I had trouble with my engine, and needed time to fix it. I tinkered about, without much success, then found the main jet was blocked and cleared it. We decided in consequence to set off back for Urquhart Bay. It was dusk when we started, but our two boats finished the long journey together, lights glowing eerily as we rounded Castle Point, bucking through the rough water in the dark.

I had grown to accept the company of Ivor's boat, and its cheerful occupant, and when he and the Petersons left the scene of operations Urquhart Bay seemed a very empty place. I knew Ivor would be back later, but in the meantime I was alone on the water again at night.

The deserted shoreline at Loch Ness has a character which varies from place to place. It can be tranquil and secure, or black and foreboding, and exposed to every squall; and at one place in particular, a mile-long deserted stretch, I experienced a curious sensation of unease at night. This was so powerful I had to force myself to overcome it, and so real I mentioned it to people at the LNI and also Mrs Cary, who has a long experience of the Ness. In her younger days she fished a great deal, and knows every yard of water locally. She told me the same stretch of water had much the same effect on her, years before, and that when rowing home she would avoid fishing there. There was something 'unpleasant' about it. Even more peculiar – a few days later by chance she happened to read a paragraph from an old book called *Urquhart and Glenmoriston: Olden Times in a Highland Parish* by William Mackay LID, which had been lent to her.

The following extract is from Chapter 21, 'Folklore in the Parish':

According to tradition the Urquhart witches were, hundreds of years ago, the bearers of the stones for the walls of Urquhart Castle. These stones were brought from the districts of Caiplich and Abriachan, and the rock from which the wretched carriers got the first sight of the castle, as they toiled towards it with their burdens, is to this day called 'Cragan nam Mallachd' – the Rock of Curses. The great place of meeting of the Urquhart witches was 'An Clarsach' – The Harp, a rock on the shore of Loch Ness and within the bounds of the farm of Tychat. There they could be seen congregated on certain nights under the presidency of his Satanic Majesty, who sat on the edge of the rock and when not engrossed in more serious business, played to them on bagpipes and stringed instruments – which circumstance gave the rock its name. . . . Their evil influence was exercised quietly and in secret and involved the objects of their attentions in misfortune or even death.

The section of shoreline which interested us is below an estate sometimes referred to as 'Cathouse' by the local people, but its official name is 'Tychat'.

I have yet to establish where the Harp Rock is, but it cannot be far from the spot where I anchored.

On 10 September Ivor and I played a part in another typical Ness experiment which had all the usual elements of drama tinged with farce. It had been decided to 'drop-test' Dan Taylor's one-man submarine in deep water, using *Lochalsh*, an old motorized barge on charter from Inverness. The idea was to lower the submarine's empty hull up and down three times to prove its integrity.

Fussy Hen, the orange lifeboat, first appeared towing the sub. out of Urquhart Bay. She was packed with a crew of young men from the LNI, mostly in frog-suits, who reminded me of the Keystone Cops. She flew three flags, incomprehensible to all but the students of the International Signal Code. They stood for 'submarine down' and, if nothing else, met the requirements of the Caledonian authority. In mid-loch the tow came to a dead stop awaiting *Lochalsh*, and Ivor and I came upon it in our boats, trailing dinghies. The temptation was too great and we circled them at full throttle, round and round, making Red Indian noises. It was one of those silly situations and set the mood for what was to follow.

Lochalsh hove in sight, gradually making up to us. We tied up alongside, and in the hours that followed the two-ton midget submarine was cranked up and down to a depth of several hundred feet. I say 'cranked', because that is exactly the right expression. Incredibly, the old gear-winch on *Lochalsh* was hand-operated, and the Keystone Cops had a great amount of cranking to do. It must have been the first time that anyone has ever wound a submarine up and down by hand.

While all this was going on, the whole collection of boats was drifting slowly down the middle of the loch, and opposite Urquhart Castle they caused a traffic jam, as visitors in hundreds peered open mouthed.

With the job done *Lochalsh* ploughed back to Inverness, leaving the submarine to hitch up a tow again, but during the test it had shipped water through the hatch and came perilously close to sinking. For a moment the situation was truly critical – saved by Ivor Newby, who abandoned his own boat, rolling backwards into the icy water in his frog-suit, to join in the struggle to connect an airline. His boat was still motoring when I lassoed it. I think his quick action saved *Viperfish* which was blown clear of water, and de-ballasted on the spot by throwing rocks out through the conning tower, a most peculiar sight to watch.

Later that afternoon, I became involved in a film-shooting sequence for Scottish TV, who wanted to do a piece on *Water Horse* for a new programme called 'One over the eight'. Stewart Henry, the disc jockey, was to put the questions, and as the sun came out brilliantly that afternoon, instead of working from shore we moved out on to the water of the bay. The Keystone Cops again – with camera men and sound recordists, female directors and secretaries crowding aboard.

As you will probably remember the Independent Television News people did a long interview some weeks back, so I had no qualms. TV work is always interesting, and the people equally so.

Later that evening I met Bob Love, the American, who had arrived to start sonar operations in *Rangitea* which has moved into the bay. Work started at once to fit her out with the mass of electronic and sonar gear, and I was soon invited aboard to look around.

Preparations for the sonar search are now extensive, and in a few days the loch will be 'pinging' loudly, and I must pay full attention to the surface, because I feel there is just a chance the noise may pop these creatures up out of fright – either that, or down, in the other direction to hide.

Operations became so involved and tense during the last few days of the marathon I found myself spending fifteen or sixteen hours on watch each day, moving *Water Horse* about to places of advantage, and there was no time to write letters, or post them. There was barely time to go ashore for food and water. I knew the giant's hour-glass was running out for me, and determined to put in a final effort.

On 12 September, starting at daybreak, I became involved in another bizarre experiment in underwater acoustics, in company with the lifeboat, and Ivor's craft. At intervals we hove to and dropped weighted light-bulbs overboard, working to a signal code flagged between the boats. We knew these would collapse, or 'implode' at a depth of 600–700 ft, producing a noise like a pistol shot, which echoed through the loch. It all went nicely, but of the Monster there was no sign, so we turned about and motored back in rough water. I had a young American aboard as second camera man, and for a while I let him steer the boat. I stood up in the hatch for'ard, with head and shoulders poking out, watching the hiss and flow of water rushing past. It had a mesmeric effect, but I was brought back to reality by the nose of *Water Horse* burying itself in a wave, and throwing the top of it straight into my face – about a bucketful of ice water. It deflected off me and over the helmsman, but there was something ridiculously funny about it, like slipping on a banana skin, and we both laughed.

One thing about boat work on the Ness is that it creates an extraordinary *bonhomie* amongst the monster-hunters, a sort of excitement. It's like flying – I've seen this in people's faces, freedom and colour and light, all mixed up together – intoxicating. It makes up for all the physical effort and interminable lack of results, beyond the occasional scrap of film, or blip on a sonar screen. It balances the scales.

Within a day or two of this episode, Birmingham University's sonar on Temple Pier started to beam across the loch, and I was invited in to view the sonar-scopes. They were confusing, but I was told that practice quickly enables one to pick out moving objects. Boats leave a broad band of dots, reflections of bubbles off the propeller, masking the screen; and for this reason I was asked not to cut across the bay, but rather go round the perimeter in *Water Horse*.

The sonar search was intensified when the Plessey team in *Jessie Ellen* put out one morning, and set up a loud underwater noise. One could even hear it on the surface, and the racket underwater was earsplitting; a high-pitched pinging sound. On two mornings this was augmented by rattles, towed along the bottom from either end of the loch by boats: *Scot II*, the converted tug-boat from Inverness, and *Vigilant*, a pleasure cruiser from Fort Augustus. The rattles were of the type used by naval ships to mislead acoustic torpedoes homing in on them.

The whole operation was intended to drive whatever was under-water through the Birmingham sonar screen, where it would duly be recorded; but it did not have this effect, and because of the blanket coverage given on television news, this failure produced an anticlimax. But it did not, in my opinion prove, or disprove any-thing. I was there, on the spot, throughout these operations, watch-ing from *Water Horse* and it struck me forcibly how *local* they were. The vast expanse of Loch Ness, stretching to east and west was unaffected.

This point was brought home to me shortly before my departure, when I left Urquhart Bay one jelly-calm morning, and idled down to Foyers, where a trawler skipper had reported seeing *two* monsters on the surface together the day before. As soon as I left the Bay I realized how small it was in fact – like a children's playground, with all the activity and excitement – only a twentieth part of the surface water, the rest of which remained as empty and undisturbed as I had found it in *Cizara* the year before.

I anchored just off *The Island*, and on the way back, surfing in rough water, just a lonely dot, I realized how much I had become a water animal. There was no fear.

I went ashore that evening at Temple Pier, and was interested to see a strange vessel pull into the bay, flying the Stars and Stripes. One gets used to the occasional big ocean-going craft, or giant trimaran anchoring for the night, but this craft had the news-men in a tizzy. Could it be a pirate press-boat, out to scoop their story?

When it was dark, they had a look at her through an electronic light intensifier, which extraordinary piece of equipment had been brought in to aid the Nessie-hunt. I had a peep through it myself and was astonished to see the boat in detail, just as though it was daylight. There was an artificial greenish glow about the image, which of course was projected on a cathode-ray tube, but when you looked away from the eyepiece the night was pitch-black. The contrast was dramatic, but it did not reveal any secret activity aboard – and early the next morning, when out by the castle I watched a small boat pull away, and row over slowly. A young boy was pulling at the oars, which were so much too large for him that he had to stand up to them. A middle-aged lady sat in the stern. The light was from the far shore and threw them into picturesque silhouette, against the glassy water and the Castle Tower. A lovely effect, and when they came near I found the boat was an old one, heavy and clinker-built with the name *Windflower* carved in elegant scroll-work at the bow. I invited them alongside, and we talked a little. The lady was a Scot, and the boy an American. They told me their big sailing boat was originally built as a Norwegian prawn-trawler, and this accounted for the upsweep of the hull and the great width of beam – reminding one of a Norseman's galley. Anything less like a 'pirate press-boat' one could not imagine, but I suppose its unusual appearance and late arrival the evening before had made it a talking point.

Oddly enough, at about this time in the hunt, I had another puzzling experience when anchored for the night, under the western shoreline. It was dark, but with a sheen on the water. I had just turned in, and lay half propped up in my bunk when I saw a bright white light in the sky perhaps 2 or 3 miles away. It did not flash like an aircraft navigation light, but varied in intensity, a sort of pulsation, at about 3,000 ft. It then moved up into the cloud which it illuminated like a Chinese lantern, before disappearing to reappear momentarily some distance away.

It was real, and did not behave like a plane or helicopter, of that I am certain; so what was it? I remember thinking to myself – 'one mystery at a time please!'

With the passage of time the hunt drew inexorably to its conclusion. At first there had been so much time I scarcely thought about it, the days and weeks blending into each other. But now I was faced with the reality of failure. In ten years of relentless effort, and through eighteen expeditions I had not been able to improve on the film I shot in 1960. I had been close to the Beast on several occasions, of that I was certain, judging by the water disturbances which could not otherwise be explained, but these did not constitute proof. I wanted close-up film, but knew inwardly that I was not going to get it.

I had watched the season change from summer to autumn and one afternoon with little *Water Horse* riding peacefully at anchor close to the ancient castle ruin, a flutter of coloured leaves drifted down on to the water, like teardrops. It was a sombre moment for me.

I stood for a long time in thought, the ice cold of the water conducting through the hull, freezing my feet. Nature is so poignant, so inexpressibly beautiful on occasion that it holds a message for us, a form of visual poetry, rare fragments of which have been contained in verse. 'He leadeth me beside the still waters' – the words of the Old Testament poet. The hours went by, and as the evenings were closing in I withdrew to the shelter of the cabin.

Of one thing I was now absolutely certain. On an individual basis, the odds against a repeated sighting were so long that one could not count on defeating them. I had proved this. I might succeed in the next ten minutes, or perhaps not for *another* ten years. That was the measure of it – and as my whole private expedition effort hinged on the assumption that one man working efficiently, with the best equipment, for a long period, could probably beat the odds, the sooner I admitted this mistake the better.

But, as the Monsters were still alive, and active, judging by my own experience during the summer, with wakes and disturbances, and sighting reports from people in boats who had been close enough not to be mistaken – if there was a solution at all it must lie in the technical approach; the sort of communal effort put up by the LNI and the other scientific groups.

The morning of 21 September dawned clear, but the sunrise had a deep cherry hue to it, reminding me of the day on which I nearly lost *Cizara*. I took note of it because I have learned to read the sky like the Ancient Mariner, and at 12 o'clock I up-anchored and moved across the bay to bid farewell to the sonar and submarine people, the LNI crews and all the other friends I had made. The sonar work was still in progress, and would continue in *Rangitea* for two or three weeks yet so a lot depended on Bob Love's coming efforts.

I settled down to the long journey back to Inchnacardoch, the rain hissing in torrents, the water glassy, but I could not forget the ominous sunrise. Cherry-red meant trouble. Wind in all probability;

and two hours later it arrived. Up till then the journey had been uneventful, with magnificent swathes of rain and mist shrouding the mountains, but I was numb with cold and, with several inches of water in the cockpit, had lost contact with my feet. I dropped anchor near Cherry Island, and went ashore to find Ivor waiting for me in his bright red sports car. He whisked me back to Urquhart Bay, where I picked up the Jaguar. I was too tired and cold to extricate the boat, but was determined to spend this last night – the eighty-second – aboard. In the meantime I visited the MacDonalds at Inchnacardoch Hotel, who kindly treated me to dinner. The warmth and comfort of the hotel was inviting but outside the massive stone building the wind was roaring through the trees, which bent and swayed together. It was more than a gale, and I realized the danger. Down the restricted cleft formed by the walls of the loch the wind could reach hurricane force, and any small boat that drifted out would be either sunk or pounded on the rocks.

I had to get back to *Water Horse*. The surface of Inchnacardoch Bay was protected but to reach the boat I would need to use the rubber dinghy. The wind and the noise were unnerving. I moved out upwind, to allow for the drift, making an interception, then climbed on board, nosing *Water Horse* right up under the trees, almost into the mud. All round me in the bay I saw strange whitish blobs in the dark and, wondering if it was wreckage, turned on the blazing spotlight. The bay was full of wildfowl taking shelter. They showed no sign of alarm, which proves that in extraordinary natural circumstances animals lose their fear of man.

As I had become so much a water animal myself, I felt at home with them and huddled down in my bunk to sleep – but as so often happens on Loch Ness the wind dropped as suddenly as it started, and I rose to a tranquil dawn. It hardly seemed possible; the whole experience was unreal – as though it had never happened – and yet all about lay the wreckage from the wind the night before. Boats sunk, or broken from their moorings, branches down, and ancient trees uprooted. The whole episode has taught me a lesson, that at Loch Ness no one can entirely master the environment.

11
'a'Mhorag' and the bog kelpies

Approximately mid-way through the expedition in *Water Horse* in 1969 something extraordinary happened, which made national news on television, and in the press. It concerned Loch Morar, situated about 40 miles to the west of Loch Ness close to the craggy Western Highland seaboard. It is the deepest known loch in Scotland, at 170 fathoms. Morar also has clear water and many shallow places, and is a mere 11 miles in length – but it too had been an arm of the sea in quite recent times, geologically.

The nature of this event, or the first garbled account of it to reach my ears, seemed to indicate a hoax, and I treated it as such, bearing in mind the recently reported find of a colossal 'dinosaur'-type bone on the shores of Loch Ness. This had also made the headlines, but when the facts became more obvious concerning the origins of the bone, the excitement it caused dissolved away into laughter.

But Loch Morar, I knew, had for long carried its own monster story, and background of history referred to by Constance Whyte in *More Than a Legend*, indicating the presence of animals similar to those reported in Loch Ness, and having their own nickname. In Gaelic this was a'Mhorag – a name used in the past by older local people, some of whom attributed the omen of death to it. When the Monster was seen, a McDonell or Gillies living thereabouts would die. At a more mundane level, in English, the Monster had also been referred to as 'Morar Maggie', and in the new report the press had plumped for 'Morag', in simplification.

Loch Morar had in fact produced a very clear monster sighting report in 1964, published on 31 May in Scotland's *Sunday Post*. In this Mr Alec Patmore, a company director, and his wife Carol described seeing a live animal in perfect visibility and flat calm, exposing three large humps and some 30–40 feet of body.

H

Again it was a *Sunday Post* account which I first read on 24 August 1969, under the title 'Here's Morag the Timid Monster' and supported by a picture, a dramatic artist's impression which the *Sunday Post* claimed had been accepted by the witnesses.

Intrigued by what I read – for the encounter involved two fishermen in a small boat who collided with a huge water animal exceeding 30 ft in length – I decided to try and find out more about the incident. It was not possible to leave Loch Ness, because of my commitment to stand by Dan Taylor's submarine when diving, but within three months I had obtained enough information to form an opinion on the subject.

The first report came from Alan Dance, who was LNI group-commander at the time, and who travelled to Loch Morar to interview the witnesses. In this he was not entirely successful, but his letter of 6 December made interesting reading. I knew Alan well, and trusted his judgment.

December 9th, 1969

Dear Tim,

The episode at Loch Morar in August certainly was fascinating, all the more so for me, as I heard the story virtually at first hand, and in the vicinity of its occurrence. I had been intending for some time to go up to the loch during my stay in Scotland, and so my trip there was made all the more interesting, following the accounts which appeared in the National Press.

I arrived at Loch Ness on the morning of August 8th and the following Monday set off for Loch Morar, accompanied by Bill Smallfield, a Canadian. On arrival our first aim was to find somewhere to stay, as near as possible to the Loch itself. We therefore motored down the narrow winding road to Bracora, and were immediately successful in finding a 'Bed and Breakfast' place, commanding a fine view of the small islands at the western end of the Loch, and as far east as Brinacory. Our luck in finding such a convenient base was augmented when we discovered that our host a Mrs Parks was in fact the sister of Duncan McDonell, one of the men involved in the incident. The garden at the back of the house led straight down to the Loch, and a few yards out was moored a small motor boat. This was the boat in which the encounter with the creature took place, and it was from here that the two men had set off for their fishing trip and to which they later hurriedly returned. Unfortunately we were not able to meet the two men concerned, Duncan McDonell and William Simpson, as both were lorry drivers and were away most of the time we were there. We did however hear the whole story of their encounter from Mrs. Parks who was the first person to meet them when they returned from that eventful fishing trip.

On the evening of Saturday August 16th, they were returning from the head of the Loch, when they saw a 'pole like' object approaching them behind. That this was animate (presumably the head and neck) they had no doubt. The animal then came alongside the boat, knocking against it and rocking it so that a small stove in the cabin on which a kettle was boiling, was overturned, Simpson immediately went to right this, whilst McDonell grabbed an oar, and literally tried to lever the creature away from the boat. It was in the act of doing this that the end of the oar broke – the oar was NOT bitten off by the creature, as reported in some Newspaper accounts. Simpson then came back on deck, and fired a ·22 over the top of the creature. Immediately it submerged and was not seen again.

Mrs. Parks described how frightened the pair were when they arrived back at the house, and her total sincerity in telling the story could not be doubted. They had certainly had a nasty shock. What was further convincing was that Simpson and McDonell had evidently been the first to scoff when other people had reported seeing 'Morag', furthermore, they did not want the press to get hold of the story, and were rightly annoyed when a few days later it was leaked to one of the Scottish nationals.

Later in the week Bill had to leave, but I was joined by David Scott, another old campaigner at Loch Ness. During the next few days, we explored as much as possible of the shores of Loch Morar, and managed to interview two other locals who had had sightings. The first was John McVarish, an inhabitant of Morar. He had had a very good one, head and neck sighting in August 1968, whilst out fishing near the islands. On August 11th 1969, he was again out

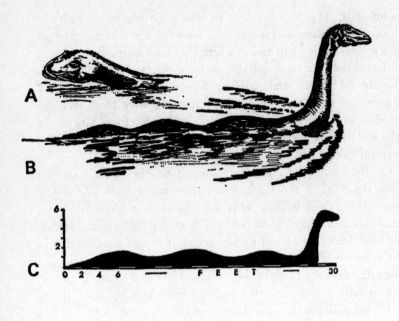

Figure 8   Sketches A and B are accurately based on the artist's impression of 'Morag' published in Scotland's Sunday Post, 24 August 1969; as approved by witnesses – 'how the head looked to Mr McDonell as he saw it from the boat' – '30 ft. from head to end of third hump' – 'dark brown skin with pebbled appearance; [body] about 5–6 feet broad; [neck] 5–6 feet long about 1 foot in diameter broadening to 2 feet, dark brown skin like sandpaper' – 'head 2 ft. long wedge-shaped like monk fish'.

Sketch C shows outline of Monster scaled to meet these comments, and a reported hump height of 2 feet above water level.

Sketch D shows three humps drawn by Mr R. H. Lowrie, seen at close range on Loch Ness from his yacht Finola, in 1961. Animal's length estimated at 30–40ft.

fishing in the vicinity of the islands, this time accompanied by a Mr. James Hanratty. It was the latter who first spotted the three-humped object, travelling very fast between the islands about 500 yards away. They closed in on it but it disappeared behind one of the islands, about 5 minutes later they saw a wake, 'like that from an outboard motor' coming towards them, and passing the boat at a distance of about 20 yards, again, in telling the story, Mr. McVarish was absolutely convincing. He treated the whole matter with an almost complete unconcern, almost as if it were an everyday occurrence. He had not been frightened, only curious, he had known of the existence of these creatures since he was a child, he was an experienced fisherman on the Loch, and unlikely to be fooled by any normal phenomenon. He had several times seen peculiar wake patterns and disturbances in the Loch, but only twice had he actually seen the creatures and both times at a close enough range for him to be absolutely certain that what he had seen was animate, but unlike any animal that he had ever seen or heard of before.

The other witness was a Mr. John Gillies, the local school taxi driver. In all his time spent in the vicinity of the Loch, he had had just one sighting about 15 years ago, of the 'upturned boat' variety again at the western end of the Loch.

Whilst we were at Loch Morar, we did hear of other local people who had had sightings, but were unable to go any further in investigating these reports, mainly for the want of time.

The thing that impressed me most about the accounts we had heard was the matter of fact approach in which they were told. There was no attempt to exaggerate or glamorise, and we had to ask many questions in order to get what information we did. It seems that these creatures are simply accepted by the locals as being there, and that is that. Generally sightings do not get reported in the press because the witnesses do not let the stories leak out. This I think is the reason why so few people have heard of 'Morag'. Loch Morar is a very lonely and isolated place, its shores are only accessible by car on the north side for about one and a quarter miles, and there are only a handful of houses within sight of it, because of this, most of the accounts come from the local fishermen and by nature they do not talk much about what they have seen.

But from what we were able to find out, I left with no doubt in my mind about the authenticity of the stories and of the existence in Loch Morar of some large animate beings. Certainly Loch Morar is worthy of further investigation.

Yours, etc.,
Alan

Almost immediately after receiving this letter, I was able to contact David Scott, who I had met some years previously, and chatted to him on the telephone. He had interviewed both Simpson and McDonell in person, obtaining sightings reported for the LNI, which were of course signed by these witnesses. He was kind enough to send me their accounts with a covering note.

December 15th 1969

Dear Tim,

So sorry for the delay in sending an account of the Morar incident. I was really waiting for the LNI sighting reports which I gave them [i.e. McDonell and Simpson]. I enclose a photostat of one [Duncan McDonell] and here is what the report of William Simpson's says. 'As we were sailing down the loch in my boat we were suddenly disturbed and frightened by a thing that surfaced behind us. We watched it catch us up and bump into the side of the boat. The impact sent a kettle of water which was heating on a gas stove to the floor, I ran into the cabin to turn the gas off as the water had put out the flame. I then came out of the cabin to see my mate try to fend the beast off with an old oar. To me he was wasting his time, then when I saw the oar break I grabbed my rifle and quickly putting a bullet in it I fired in the direction of the beast. I then watched it slowly sink away from the boat, and that was the last I saw of it.'

When I spoke to the witnesses a fortnight after the incident, both appeared embarrassed and unwilling to speak. It took some time to draw them out, occasionally one would contradict the other on a point of detail. I cannot believe that if their story was a complete hoax they would behave in this way.

One of them told me as a small boy, he and a group of young friends had seen something very strange moving in the loch one day

when they were returning home from school, on telling his parents
he was firmly rebuked for telling such terrible 'fibs'.

Do ring me if you want any further information.

David Scott

Duncan McDonell's description reads as follows:

My friend and I were travelling down Loch Morar in our boat, we
were moving quite slowly at the time, I was preparing a cup of tea
when I heard a splash or disturbance in the water astern of us, I
looked up and about twenty yards behind us this creature was
coming directly after us in our wake, it only took a matter of seconds
to catch up on us, it grazed the side of the boat. I am quite certain
this was unintentional. When it struck the boat it seemed to come
to a halt or at least slow it down. I grabbed the oar and was attempting to fend it off, my one fear being that if it got under the boat it
might capsize it. I struck it with the oar quite hard breaking the
oar in doing so, then I heard a report at my side, my friend had fired
a shot. The noise seemed to scare it and it dived into the depths.
After our ordeal we went ashore and this is when I really realized the
dangerous position we had been in, it was really very nerve-racking.

David James's newsletter about the LNI's summer activities included
the following paragraph:

I heard about the incident the following Monday, and motored
straight up. By this time McDonell, a long distance lorry driver,
was away in Glasgow, but it was quite clear that Simpson
had had a very nasty fright indeed. I have not yet met
McDonell but by all accounts his story tallied, and I find it
inconceivable that any two people should publish a hoax at a
time when they were 150 miles from each other, and could not
rely on mutual corroboration.

As a further check on details, an unsolicited letter from the
Island of Lewis provided a breakdown on all the Morar sightings,

and included a map showing where these had occurred. Upon writing to its author, a Mr Donald Gilliland who toured the island's schools as an art instructor, I found another private investigator who had taken the trouble to examine the case. These letters left me in no doubt as to the reality, and therefore the *importance* of the reports from Morar.

I already knew of two cases at Loch Ness where the Monster was said to have come up under boats, almost capsizing them; one case where two animals were seen alongside, making a hissing noise; and two cases where it surfaced close enough to cause anxiety. Not all of these reports were documented, but hearsay can be accurate in substance if inaccurate in detail.

The one common factor in all these reports was the fear experienced by witnesses, in some cases amounting almost to terror – causing a local salmon fisherman to give up his lucrative hobby until his courage slowly returned, a lonely oarsman at night to 'shout his head off' at the Beast, hoping to frighten it away, and a sail-ferry boatman to stop ferrying altogether.

My own experience in *Water Horse* at night had proved uneasy, and once I had been genuinely afraid when an inexplicable wake-arm pattern with foot-high waves had rocked the boat.

But I was not ashamed of this reaction – indeed I felt a trifle smug when ticking it off my mental list, as 'proven'. In the event of an encounter in the dark fear would be much greater than in the daytime, and one would need to allow for it in training.

Towards the end of September 1969 there was a gradual exodus from the Loch Ness hunting-grounds, but some of the more intrepid quite literally moved camp to a bog on the west coast of Ireland, in County Galway.

Captain Lionel Leslie, a cousin of Sir Winston Churchill, had been the first Nessie-hunter to switch his sights to the loughs of Ireland, in search of what appeared to be aquatic animals similar to those reported in the Ness, and Morar, but of smaller size.

Later he was joined by Ted Holiday, and others who became interested in his experiments and plans to try and catch one. Ivor Newby, Chris Elmer, and Holly Arnold from the resident LNI staff at the Achnahannet site made up the party. Captain Leslie had obtained the necessary permits to net three small lakes joined by streams, with a single outlet running to the sea.

These proved to be very shallow, with a layer of ooze beneath, and for a period of a month some 500 ft of special nets were put out, or trolled slowly, but without result.

Subsequently, on 17 November 1969, the *Western Mail* published an article by its angling correspondent entitled 'Irish Angle on the Monster' describing their experiences. The writer, F. W. (Ted Holiday kept very much to the point:

> The biggest of the lakes was a mile or more long, and the smallest about half a mile. Plumbing them was the first job. We expected considerable depth but found to our surprise that nowhere were they deeper than about eight feet. Our aqualung diver, Ivor Newby, however, reported that there was a great depth of soft ooze, and he was unable to plough down far enough to touch hard bottom.
>
> Meeting and checking witnesses was an important part of the operation. Mr W. J. Wood, the director of a timber company, told me, 'At all times I had the impression of a kind of snake-like object – an eel-like object, shall I say, with the head very much resembling a calf.'
>
> Tom Joyce, the farmer on whose land we were operating, saw a specimen in 1964. 'At first there was only a small section in view', he told us. 'Then it got bigger until eventually it was about seven or eight feet long.' This portion had stood about two feet out of the water, and was moving. Mr Joyce saw it crush its way through some reeds before it finally submerged.
>
> Another farmer, about a mile away, described how a neck and head appeared beside the boat while he was fishing, causing him to row ashore in haste. Yet another man told us how, when he was a boy, he was collecting peat with his mother. They both saw a large creature showing several humps which seemed to have a mane on its neck. It looked rather like a gigantic eel.
>
> I had the nets specially made by Messrs. Middleton of Grimsby. They were of 1 ft. square mesh with each strand breaking at 350 lb. The material was polystyrene, a rot-proof

synthetic. Such a net would hold a shark or a bull elephant. They were of various sizes but mostly 50 feet long by 20 feet deep.

In view of the shallowness of the lakes we decided to cut the nets in half lengthwise, and thus double our effective coverage. A visit to local garages yielded several hundredweights of scrap-iron with which the nets were weighted. The tops of these nets were supported by yellow plastic buoys, six inches in diameter.

The weather was stormy and wet. During our month in the bog there were only four dry days. This did nothing to make the work easy or pleasant, especially as we had no facilities for drying our clothes.

By October 11th we had managed to put nearly 500 feet of net into the three loughs. Using a motorboat, we had also tried a sort of trawling operation. Holly suggested using butchers offal as bait, and a messy experiment on these lines was tried. Gales swept the bog repeatedly, and on many days it was impossible to get afloat. There was water everywhere, and when Irish television arrived to record our adventure, they had to hold umbrellas over the cameras.

After some weeks of this, with November approaching, it was wise to admit defeat. The nets were recovered and stored, and there was time to take stock.

Almost every sighting of the creatures had been in fine warm conditions.

Ted Holiday had invited me to join the Irish expedition – but I had been on Loch Ness for such a long time I needed a rest, and I wanted to get back to my family. As it turned out it was the bad weather which spoiled their undertaking, though it did not stop them from accomplishing what they had set out to do. I admired their pluck, and especially that of the females in the party, Holly and Chris, both of whom were true expeditioners. On Loch Ness Chris had won Ivor Newby's and my respect by cooking meals for us in Urquhart Bay, despite rough weather, and rain and the lack of space. Always cheerful, we bestowed upon her the unusual nickname of 'Boat Moppet' and were referred to jointly in return as 'Monster Men'. I suspect that inwardly we came to cherish these rather foolish titles, which seemed to fit in with our surroundings and our faintly idiotic mode of existence – and like so many nick-names, they stuck.

During the Irish adventure I felt the urge to correspond in verse, and posted a few stanzas, little realizing how prophetic these would turn out to be.

They went something like this:

ODE TO THE BOG-KELPIE HUNTERS

Boat Moppet – Boat Moppet
  are you back home
    or did the Bog-kelpies get you
abroad when you roamed?

With Ivor, and Ted, and Holly the fair
  with bold Captain Leslie
    in Bog-kelpie's Lair

With nets, all embracing
  and so many floats
    there was really no need
to bother with boats,

As you closed in around it
  and gave a loud SHOUT
    to frighten the Kelpie
and make it POP OUT!

But if it laid doggo,
  and tricked you the while
    as brave Kelpie-hunters
no doubt you did smile

As back to old Blighty
  the five of you flit
    in no way depress-ed
no, no, not a bit

And remember Boat Moppet
  that no matter 'wot
    some day we will trap one
if not a whole lot –
  so chin up, and Bonzo
    be bright as you can
      when you scribble a verse
to old Monster Man.

In due course I had a reply, in verse, on an immense Irish postcard glowing with emerald greensward, and portraying Bally-something-or-other Castle.

Reading between the lines I got the impression that life had not been too kind, with the constant rainfall, and the quaking bog beneath, on which their tents had quite literally been floating. Later, Ivor told me that the Moppet, for all her natural buoyancy had failed two important tests – the 'Water in Tent' test, and the 'Rats in Tent' test, the latter quite miserably. A severe view was taken of this at the time and there had been talk of a drumhead court-martial, but in view of the weather the idea had to be abandoned, along with the tents.

With their return from Ireland, only Bob Love's team in *Rangitea* remained actively monster-hunting on Loch Ness. But on 10 October 1969, they scored a bull's-eye – a discrete record of sonar blips appearing on the target screen, the apparent acoustic reflections from some very large object several hundred feet beneath the surface, which steered a loop course, altering both speed and depth as they tracked it.

The effect this would have on all our lives in 1970 could not then be estimated.

12
Nessie in '70

During the off-season following the escapade in *Water Horse* there was much to be done. The LNI had invited me to run the fieldwork the following summer as surface photography director. This meant being at Loch Ness for an even longer period – for up to five months, and a departure from the solitary hunting which had always been my *forte*. In contrast, life would be jam-packed with variety and human contact. It would mean working from Achnahannet, the LNI's basecamp and training teams and individuals throughout the summer.

The prospect of doing this was sobering. I was not certain that I could stand the pace of so long an expedition. In the past the group-commanders had found they were exhausted after only two weeks of it. I had never tackled anything quite like it – and perhaps for this reason more than any other, I said 'yes' to the job.

Throughout the winter months, the task of planning and organizing became a matter of reality. By now I knew many of the expeditioners, and had contacts which would be useful, and in November I travelled out to Norfolk, to the country home of a man who was famous for his work on autogyros – Wing Commander K. H. Wallis, CEng, AFRAeS. I knew of him from my days in aeronautics, and had seen him demonstrate his tiny one-man machines at the Farnborough air show. After a service career in the RAF Ken Wallis had turned his mind and engineering skills to the science of designing, and building his own autogyros; and had since gained an international reputation and two world records for the type.

At Reymerston Hall, deep in the flat-lands of East Anglia, I watched fascinated as he took off from his own front lawn, about the size of a pair of tennis courts, and zoom round the sky and the tree-tops in a dazzling display of exhibition flying. Later, in company with Ivor Newby, who was also an ex-RAF pilot, we were shown his workshops, and the 'gyro sheds outside, in which he kept nine of these machines.

Perhaps the most impressive part of the exhibition had been the autogyro's stability in very rough air conditions. The rotating wing, or gyro blades above the pilot did not react to turbulence in the way a glider's wing would do. Due to their rate of revolution buffeting did not cause the tilting inherent in a glider.

As a result of this demonstration, and with the support of David James at the LNI, who was an optimist, a contract was signed for Wing Commander Wallis to patrol Loch Ness. He would stand off at several thousand feet, then throttle back and spiral in to shoot film of any monster target which presented itself. To do this effectively he would need to silence the exhaust to some extent, and to develop an operating technique which suited the conditions.

In the late spring of 1970, when plans had advanced, I travelled up to Loch Ness by overnight sleeper, awaking to find orange sunlight gleaming off the mountain snowscape. The train, ascending a gradient, seemed reluctant to disturb the solitude; the click of its metal muted, the chill of its corridors refreshing, reminding me of the winter past.

At Inverness, I was met by one of the young men from Achnahannet, and driven out to inspect the site and the battered caravans, staring emptily at the icy loch beneath, vast and silent. The camp had been in use through five summer expeditions, increasing in size from a single caravan to the half dozen green painted shells which made up the accommodation. It was not a model base, and yet it served a purpose and throughout the monster-hunting season it became alive with people and ideas – a focal point for operations.

Prospects of this occurring again were good, but at the time I could only guess at what would happen, and retreated hurriedly to search out new commanding sites for the long-range cameras. The search took us up into the mountains, along the dizzy logging roads built by the forestry commission, in places almost 1,000 ft sheer above the loch and providing a balance of perspective; and later, back at home in the south I made the final preparations for what would prove to be one of the most interesting and exhausting experiences of a lifetime.

Notes on the shore and surface watch in '70

From: The Surface Photography Director
To: Loch Ness Investigation Bureau Ltd.
Date: 1.1.71

In 1970 for the first time the two main arms of the LNI – the above-surface photography and the underwater research, operated separately, under autonomous control but with a high degree of mutual aid and understanding. To put it briefly – we got on well together, and between us added something to the gradually accumulating store of knowledge. This report is concerned with the 'above surface' part of the hunt.

For the photographers, 'Nessie in '70' started officially on Saturday 23 May, when the first and now almost traditional senior crew was able to start work effectively, and with the best of good humour. This group was at Achnahannet for a week, and thereafter teams replaced each other at the usual fortnightly intervals running through twenty-one weeks to 17 October.

It did not take long to find that the petty annoyances of malfunctioning equipment, water in the petrol, 'dead' batteries and so on were no real deterrent, and before long the operation was running smoothly on a two-level duty basis, with good test photography resulting, and the best of comradeship; and with the spectrum of skills available to us through the flow of expeditioners we became progressively better at the job.

Public relations

A vast concourse of people of all nationalities visited the PR caravan – individuals, groups, families, coach-loads of Europeans, Japanese and Americans filtered through it. Financial intake was a record, despite our decision to drop the entry price from two and sixpence, to two shillings (adults) and one shilling (children). This was in large part due to the good stocks of literature made available, and the calmly efficient control exercised by Jeff Hepple, the most senior member of the resident voluntary staff.

At the technical level, visits were paid by various important people in the fields of zoology, biology, nature conservancy and oceano-graphy – the majority of whom expressed a personal interest in the research, and a minority of whom worked in conjunction with us – though on specific studies not directly connected with the 'phenomena'. Because of the unique character of the loch, its fluid environment, and physical structure it may prove in time to be a focal point for field studies.

Harbour project

Due to the vulnerability of workboats on any main stretch of Loch Ness, the need for some form of protection was obvious. We have in consequence built a small but effective harbour structure on the foreshore below Achnahannet. This was accomplished at virtually no cost by expeditioners with wetsuits, who rafted boulders in, 'bombing' them into position using face-masks. Perhaps 100 tons of rock has been moved in this manner, and although the finishing touches have yet to be made, our 'HQ Harbour' is already in service, and proven in gales of up to 100 m.p.h. When the loch floods, however, it disappears from sight.

Fishing

Great efforts were made to catch or capture eels using long-lines of traditional pattern, and some ingenious traps. A number of big hooks were taken, indicating powerful eels, but unlike the under-water research contingent who did catch some very interesting eel specimens, the LNI has yet to score off Achnahannet. However, giant-eel fever is as catching as the quarry is elusive, and hopes are high for '71.

Beachcombing

Before *Fussy Hen*, the hefty clinker-built LNI workboat was moved to Urquhart Bay for underwater research we used her as a photo target (2 ft black and white squares being painted on her sides) and to tow in baulks of timber, and other interesting flotsam to help in the harbour project. This proved a popular and rewarding diversion.

Voluntary marooning patrols
Due to the dreadful weather persisting right through the season from the end of June, only one such patrol was mounted, on my inflatable outboard dinghy *Moo-scow*, with the LNI's hard-working and reliable helper, Rip Hepple, departing into the sombre distance. It was three days before we caught sight of him again – a tiny dot bobbing on the water but despite the cold, and drenching rainfall he had, being of a hardy disposition, enjoyed his time alone on the precipitious south-western shoreline.

Solitary patrols of this kind, which probe the quiet deep regions of the loch have a quality of their own, and a real photo potential; but one must accentuate the need for caution. A capsize, or injury ashore could result in death from exposure because of the general lack of rescue boats. Signal flares are essential, but even these can go unnoticed from behind the screen of trees of the north shore road. For this reason such patrols must never include the in-experienced – to whom they most commonly appeal.

Air patrols and ground support
Photo potential is no longer in doubt and the means of support is within the compass of the LNI, thanks to the co-operation of local farmers and landowners – and Shell-BP, who put up the fuel. Within 24 hours of Ken Wallis's arrival for the first period of operations in June, we obtained permission to use three private fields for landing and take-off.

Due to the amazing 'towability' of this tiny aircraft, the complete nature of the kit, and the immensely sporting competence of the pilot . . . it can go anywhere, anytime, and has the unique potential of plan (looking down) photography – and indeed of actually peering into the depths.

I

Loch Morar mini-expedition

In August a pilot venture including the photography boat *Water Horse*, the autogyro, and a support vehicle, travelled to Morar by the single track motor road, arriving in the usual deluge of rain. However, unlike Loch Ness in the east, the weather cleared, and we enjoyed five days of surface and aerial investigation *par excellence*. Friendly relations were established with the Morar Survey Team, whose scientific and historical report has recently been published. Loch Morar is privately owned, steeped in legend and Monster Lore – and would appear to contain a population of unknown aquatic animals similar to that of Loch Ness – if just regard is paid to the eye-witness reports of it.

Our mini-expedition was valuable, with Ken Wallis shooting dramatic, low-level movie films from the autogyro, using *Water Horse* as a target.

Long-range photography

The 'big-guns' of the LNI number half a dozen 35mm movie cameras, with lenses varying from 17 in to 36 in in focal length. Optical power is great, but inevitably there are problems – made greater by working out of doors. Mist, rain and damp prove a constant enemy, and the need to train crew members to a standard has its problems too. But despite all this, of the five sequences of film shot on possible Monster targets, wakes or disturbances – four were squarely on target, up to a range of two miles, and three had adequate exposure control. The one sequence which could have been of real value (the watcher described a triangular hump moving through the water) was shot into the sunglaze, which plays havoc with lenses.

However, our test photography was good, and given good light and clear sightings I am confident both cameras and operators can make a job of it.

Hand cameras

Second line Bolex 16mm movie cameras, and to a lesser extent, still and 8mm cameras were taken out by people working on the foreshore, or on trips to Inverness or Fort Augustus. This is necessary, as so many sightings occur unexpectedly.

Surface-photography and sonar

After test runs in Morar, *Water Horse* was put on to Loch Ness, where in company with Ivor Newby's fast boat *Kelpie*, Bob Love's sonar boat *Rangitea* and the autogyro, some pictures were taken for the BP house magazine. After this, and several weeks of use out of the HQ Harbour I moved her down to Fort Augustus for photo-drifting, this being the quieter end of the loch.

In late September the new Klein Associates side-scan sonar was brought to Loch Ness by the Academy of Applied Science team from Massachusetts, Dr Rines, Mr Blonder and Dr Martin Klein being directly involved. After trials in Urquhart Bay where sonar contacts resulted, this equipment was put aboard *Water Horse* and trailed out of Fort Augustus. More contacts were recorded.

No photography was obtained from *Water Horse*, though a momentary head-and-neck sighting in the vicinity of Urquhart Castle, in rough water, did add some excitement to many hours of otherwise tranquil drifting.

Infra-red colour, and black-and-white photography

An experiment with the former was tried out from the Wallis auto-gyro, but failed because of on-site processing. However, this film is not difficult to handle, and future aerial work may prove of value – providing Kodak do the processing. Colours come up on the basis if IR reflectivity, and haze penetration is good.

The small but enthusiastic Black & White Scotch (sponsored) expedition, working in association with the LNI principally through Bob Love's underwater section, concentrated on the latter type of IR photography, using a short range IR binocular camera, which was employed principally at night. Developments with tools of this kind could prove useful, but range is a problem. Assuming the Monster's nocturnal habit, IR photography has much to commend it, particularly for night drifting techniques.

Associated watching expeditions, and individuals
During the course of the summer LNI Bolex 16mm and LR (long-range) 35mm still cameras were farmed out to those who would be watching from different places, or from surface boats. This included a Fleet Air Arm sailing expedition, the skipper of a local pleasure boat in Urquhart Bay, groups of schoolboys, and competent individuals.

Interviews and tape recordings
Some good interviews were obtained from witnesses, and tape recordings made for record purposes. In two cases 'still' photos were taken, but with the usual dismal result. Excitement, incorrect exposure and unfamiliar cameras combined to defeat the photographer. In one case where two animals were reportedly photographed on the surface in good light, in colour, at only a short distance, the film lead strip tore on the sprocket, resulting in no wind-on or exposure whatsoever. Chance photography by amateurs has to date produced the best and worst of the still photo evidence – and will probably continue to do so.

Press and TV
During the summer the LNI co-operated with the many and persistent representatives of the national and local press, and with Italian and Norwegian TV teams, in making films and documentaries. Arrangements to assist Japanese TV (NTV) over a two-week period in making of a film did not come to fruition – but although the press and TV are always welcome the LNI has a job to do, and this takes priority.

Optical search equipment
Thanks to the gift of binoculars, telescopes and tripods from a well-wisher, the observation stations this year had a much improved scan.

Expedition health
Notwithstanding the difficulties posed by numbers, the weather,

cramped quarters and the inevitable lack of 'mod cons' health remained remarkably good: there being only one case of chicken-pox, one broken arm, one broken leg, one carbuncle, one crushed thumb, one case of lacerations caused by rusty barbed wire while-falling-down-a-cliff, one lightning strike inducing a nasty shock to the photo director through the handle of his umbrella – and one car crash causing near heart-failure to all concerned.

Recreational

In traditional style the various teams of Monster-hunters enjoyed 'kalys' at the Glen Urquhart Lodge, and much good cheer there, and at the 'Drum' and the 'Inchnacardoch'. Both 8mm and 16mm films were shown regularly, sound tapes played, guitars strummed, voices uplifted in song, and funny stories told. Perhaps the most rewarding part of LNI activity is the continuing cascade of good humour and wit, and the astounding variety of dialects. In the course of the season it is possible to hear English spoken in a score of different ways – and with the fabled loch itself as a back-drop the stage is set, with romantic attachments developing upon it – as a natural part of this great human drama.

Site improvements

With the end of existing site planning permission, local councillors and others met with us to discuss renewal ... an extension being granted upon certain improvements being made.

In consequence we drew up plans, obtained permission for a 30 ft extension of site area to include repositioned caravans, a new PR structure, kitchen, and *flushing toilets* – the latter an undreamed of luxury.

Standards

Thanks to the help of the local forestry commission office we were able to obtain two 30 ft flagpoles in the form of untrimmed pine-trunks, which were peeled, and erected, using war-surplus balloon cables as guys. From one we flew the now famous 'Nessie Pennant', of the LNI, and from cross-trees on the other the Union Jack, and the cross of St Andrew, or Saltire, as it is referred to by the Scots. These three handsome standards were flown as high as we could get them.

In conclusion

My thanks are due to the many individual crew members, the group commanders, the voluntary resident staff – and the local people, without whose help and friendship no progress could be made.

13
The human
element

In 1971 I again ran the fieldwork for the LNI, though for a period of
only four months of operations. The tremendous equinoctial gales
of the year before had convinced me of the need to 'pull stumps' by
mid-September, but, just to be awkward, Loch Ness omitted to
blow as it should have done in the autumn months. Instead, one
bright summer's afternoon when the PR information centre was
bursting with visitors it whipped up gusts which almost took the
roof off, and blew the massive HQ long-range camera rig across the
watching platform. This was so heavy it took two people just to
lift the camera and telescope off the Moy head which supported it.

It was this contraption, too, which had given the photo director a
nasty shock through the handle of his umbrella the year before, when
attempting to shield it from a downpour in a thunderstorm, a
typically barmy situation, with the GC (group-commander) of the
day assisting. He was a real Commander in fact, a distinguished
Royal Naval destroyer skipper from the Second World War, and a
great character to boot, rejoicing in the nickname 'OG'. Commander
Sir Peter Ogilvy-Wedderburn had decided to lift the camera off and
put it in a place of safety, and while doing this a thunderclap and
flash of lightning lit up the scene. The discharge was so close it
induced an electric shock through the handle of the Expedition
Umbrella which I was holding at the time, a battered relic of a
brolly, which someone had left behind in the mess.

Unnerved by this, I had suggested abandoning the equipment,
which was heavy metal, and extremely wet. In reply OG made a
comment which put him among the immortals. He said, with a broad
grin: 'It takes a few seconds for the lightning to build up again –
if we're quick, we'll make it' – and we did!

It was this attitude which characterized the expedition: a sort of good-humoured but determined optimism. It carried us through the wet, and the cold, and the attacks by countless flying insects, and the unrelenting chore of dumping toilet buckets. Indeed, the measure of unpleasantness could be counted in terms of the humour it generated. The 'Elsan' race, for example, became truly competitive, with stop watches at the ready, and stringent rules enforced. Each successive team added records to the notice board

THE GREAT ELSAN RACE
Rules
Standing start, any route, finish when elsans charged and doors closed.

Entrants
Any expedition member of either sex, or nationality, who wishes to try.
One attempt a day.

Disqualification
Dropping a bucket.
Emptying an elsan before time, and any other offence which seems to be fiddling.

First runner of 1970	Date	Record time
Ian	19 June	6 min. 5 sec.
Oglet (in fact OG's		
son Andrew)	21 June	3 min. 10 sec.
Rip	22 June	2 min. 28 sec.
Jed ('Mountain Man')		
for USA	26 June	2 min. 25 sec.

(At this place in the record an unsolicited entry appears)

'Kilroy was here'	–	32 sec.
Rip	16 Oct.	2 min. 19·8 sec.

timed by M. Barber and witnessed by 'Bear'.

This final record was admitted to be a 'damned close run thing', and no further entrants seem to have taken up the challenge; feeling perhaps that the honour of shaving further seconds off the total was outweighed by the risks.

Rip Hepple, the handyman of the LNI went on to further glory that winter by designing and building flushing loos and a cess-pit to local town and country planning standards, for which every expedition member in 1971 was to bless his name and reputation – notwithstanding that they secretly missed the elsan race.

Surprisingly, there had only been one lady to enter the race, and although her time was good, earning a prize for 'meritorious actions beyond the call of duty', for some reason her name is missing from the record.

At a more sober level, when running the fieldwork we had to make a space for all types and qualities of expeditioner, and for all age groups too. The first 'senior' crew mentioned was in fact GC'd by none other than the famous Captain Leslie – Lionel Leslie who had reached the age of 70 without losing his zest for life or poetry, or his enormous sense of humour. Lionel and OG and others of long experience captained several of the groups but in others young men took their place: mostly students from universities, or graduates with shining new degrees. The rank and file of the expeditions produced an above average IQ, and a list of budding characters. Volunteers were often from abroad and included hitch-hikers on their summer holidays, or in some cases on world-wide travels who stopped off to put in a week or two of expedition work.

Not all these people would have passed muster at a screening, but such was the enthusiasm and the general will to work that even the less fortunate among them contributed something, and were rewarded by an experience which was unique. In this way Achnahannet became a sort of staging post – a stopping-off place where good comradeship developed out of the hard work, and sometimes the tedium of watching.

The routine was simple, and each fortnight, the old crew would move out to be replaced by the new crew of volunteers. There was nothing formal about it, and until people actually arrived there was no sure means of telling how many would be on a crew. I had set the maximum at 12, and with a resident staff of 5, including myself and the occasional visitors at the evening meal we could find ourselves feeding 20 people.

On arrival, the newcomers would be shown where to sleep. Because of the long distance travelled they would often be pallid and exhausted, contrasting with the bronzed and healthy faces of the youngsters moving out. The new crew somehow always seemed inferior to the one before and yet they in turn would pull together and prove their worth, gaining confidence and ability as the days went by.

I trained them myself on the HQ camera, the huge gun-mounted telescope controlled by traverse wheels. There was a simple code of vital actions needed to get on target quickly. A time of 10 seconds from the watch office to 'camera running' was a good time, and 12 seconds the accepted average. Some individuals just could not get on target in less than 20 seconds, lacking co-ordination, but they were few in number. The majority managed well and enjoyed timing each other through the sequence until their skills improved. There were, as always, one or two brilliant operators whose drill went like a whiplash; and one or two who felt sure they could do better by doing what they liked.

Once the crews had settled down in the very early morning, depending on light and mist conditions, the GC would send out the mobile vehicles, the camera vans, to different places down the loch. These sites each had a special character, and a huge field of view over the better Monster-sighting areas, and would be manned throughout the daylight hours. In all, five main camera stations existed: HQ at Achnahannet, Foyers, Invermoriston, Basil's garage roof and Dores. There were old sites too and alternatives such as the Clansman, Quarry Brae, High or Low Dores, Temple Pier, and Fort Augustus. All these famous places were manned at one time or another through the LNI's ten-year history of monster-hunting fieldwork.

With the two-tier duty system I had introduced, watchers would spend one day on solitary camera watch, and one day back at camp on chores, manning the HQ station, the information centre, and the PR hut, through which tourists flocked in thousands.

This was always a popular diversion, and an important function, too, because it served to interest the public and bring them up to date on events; and the sale of books and reports demonstrated what had in fact been accomplished. This PR activity had started at Achnahannet almost by accident, years before, but by 1970 and 1971 it blossomed into a full-scale operation, with some 30,000, and then 50,000 visitors going through the centre. The few pence they paid on entry and the literature they bought helped to finance the expedition, which was not a cheap thing to run.

In 1970 the basic fieldwork had run on the proceeds from the PR caravan, but it had not covered the experiments – the Birmingham University sonar team, which had again come to the loch, the auto-gyro or the boat operations – but in 1971, with an enlarged PR hut to work from, a surplus was earned at Achnahannet which helped the Bureau.

Other projects like the harbour building absorbed the spare energy of the crews, and there was always plenty to be done in repairing equipment or improving camp facilities. Cooking on such a large and erratic scale was not easy to manage as there was no electricity, and only a limited supply of piped spring water, in which tadpoles might be found, but again, due to the ingenuity of a few expert cooks, and a points marker scheme for chores Achnahannet produced good meals, and an amazing variety of dishes.

The accommodation was very basic, but for all its lack of mod cons it kept the crews dry, if not in any particular comfort.

In 1970 there was a PR caravan, a watch office and business office caravan, two dormitory caravans (the Ritz for ladies, and the Black Hole for men), a mess cum cook-house caravan, a 'nuts and bolts house' workshop caravan, and a modern rented house-trailer in which I lived and used as a meeting place for visitors. In addition there was parking space for twenty cars, including the expedition's mobiles. By 1971 space had been increased, spring water had been piped to the toilets and the kitchen, and heated there by gas, and the PR hut had come into existence. Altogether Achnahannet had grown into a formidable array of vehicles.

Because of his re-election to Parliament in 1970, the LNI's executive director David James was unable to lead a team as he had done in previous years. This was unavoidable, but to be regretted because each team had a character of its own and this was influenced by the group-commander, who could either be a mature man or woman of wide experience, or a young person of unusual ability. The GCs each had something to contribute – a style, or in some cases a measure of *élan* which made them different, and their teams different too.

During the Second World War, when serving as Lieutenant aboard a Royal Navy gunboat sunk in a battle off the Hook of Holland, David James had become a POW of the Germans. After a time he decided to escape, and working on the principle that 'the best way to hide a leaf is in the forest' he walked out of the prison camp disguised as an officer in the Royal Bulgarian Navy, his forged credentials identifying him as *Ivan Bagerov*.

On the first attempt he got as far as Lübeck on the Baltic coast, but was recaptured when searching for a ship bound for neutral Sweden. He had travelled there by train, demanding assistance from the German military en route – and getting it! Later he escaped again, and using the same technique, reached Sweden, to be flown back to Britain. His book *A Prisoner's Progress* (or *Escaper's Progress* in the USA) must rank as one of the most daring and humorous escape-artist stories to have come out of the war.

Another intriguing character to be found at Achnahannet was Ken Wallis. 'Wingco Wallis' appeared first on the scene driving a Mini Cooper S., towing a trailer with the autogyro squatting neatly on it. With cans of aviation spirit on board it made a combination – a complete one-man flying kit. There was no need for a ground crew; the mini could go anywhere, and the gyro could take off from the nearest field providing it had a flat run of 100 yards or so, and a relatively unobstructed flight path.

Ken lived with the machine, and would test run the engine in the expedition car-park, surrounded by onlookers. Answering countless questions, he never lost patience and was always ready to tow out and fly off at a moment's notice. At first he had worked from Daicross airport outside Inverness, but this reduced his effective range over the loch. The solution lay in finding local take-off points, and in this we succeeded, gaining permission to fly from two of the great local estates, and from the games field of the Fort Augustus Abbey School.

The first take-off to be made away from Dalcross occurred one brilliant sunlit morning, after we had paced off distances across the stubble of a twenty-acre field, looking for hummocks of grass, and hidden rocks which might wreck the autogyro. Ken donned his flying kit and climbed into the cockpit. It was so small and at such a low angle he was almost prone in it when he started the engine and engaged the clutch to spin up the rotor. He was tall, with greying hair and a clipped moustache, and in his scarlet flying suit, helmet and goggles, he presented a striking figure. With a cheerful wave, he opened up the throttle and the strange machine lurched and bucketed off across the grass, gathering speed to lift off gracefully like some enormous insect, its whirling wings gleaming in the sunlight. With a wasplike whine from the motor he pulled up sharply to the right to clear a line of trees then circled back to fly slowly over my head. I shot film of it in colour, then turned to see an amazing sight, as incongruous as the autogyro itself.

Sailing across the countryside, with only its funnel and superstructure showing was a ship! *Scot II*, the tug-boat, passing through the Ship Canal on its way to Inverness. For a moment, I stood transfixed, calling to mind the words of the 'Brahan Seer', the Scottish prophet who had foretold that one day ships would sail across the face of the Highlands. I was looking squarely at the proof of it, and until my senses recovered enough to provide an explanation, I stood there with mouth open, staring like an idiot.

In the weeks that followed, Ken Wallis put in many hours of flying over Loch Ness, operating from the different take-off places; and I would follow him in the big Mark 8 Jaguar up and down the north shore road, conversing on radio. There was a '007' atmosphere about it, prompted by the fact that Ken had flown for one of the Bond films in the past. On one occasion too, in order to please Shell-BP, the fuel sponsors, Ivor Newby and I in *Kelpie* and *Water Horse* raced about the surface of the loch formating with the low-flying autogyro. It had little to do with monster-hunting, but was excitingly spectacular, and made good photography for the BP magazine.

At first Ken Wallis had been reserved about the Monster, but when we heard of a recent daylight sighting, and tracked down the witness in the cavernous bowels of an underground hydroelectric station – and listened to his experience, he became a determined hunter himself, rising at dawn and flying endless patrols over the water. The high-pitched whine of the autogyro soon became a common sound at the Ness; with Ken's masterful skills as a pilot, and as an air photographer, the operation proved a success. During his second stint in August of 1970 we trailed out from Achnahannet, with the Mini–gyro combination and the Jaguar towing *Water Horse*, supported by an expedition vehicle; and set off for Loch Morar some 80 miles distant by road.

It was to be an exploratory trip, but the weather was atrocious. Packing up for any expedition is hard work but to do so in the pouring rain is demoralizing. Wondering whether we should call a halt I asked Ken's opinion. He replied in a way which typified him; he said: 'If you give in to the weather on expeditions, you're pretty poorly placed.'

He was right, and after hours of squelching effort, and the long drive to Morar through mist, and some 30 miles of single track, we broke clear out into the sunlight.

For some reason, I had no particular desire to go to Loch Morar, and had a mental impression of it which proved to be mistaken. I had at first imagined a wide loch set in unimpressive scenery, although the contours on the map did not suggest this. It may have been that after years of work at Loch Ness, I could not conceive of any other loch which compared with its majestic outline, but on arriving at Morar, with Ken Wallis on a scouting trip earlier in the year, we had found it to be profoundly beautiful.

The mountains surrounding it have a mossy green-velvet texture, and a lumpiness which are absent at the Ness. The waters of Loch Morar are gin-clear, and at the broader western end the loch is shallow and dotted with islands which carry an almost primeval growth of forest and scrub.

And now, as our small cavalcade of vehicles went up past the tumbling waters of the Morar, the shortest river in the British Isles, we stopped briefly at the ancient corrugated-iron shed which served as temporary headquarters for the 'Loch Morar Survey' team, who were busily at work. The LMS, as it had already come to be known, was formed of a small committee of old-hand monster-hunters from Loch Ness, and a working group of young biologists, marine zoologists and ichthyologists, mostly from London University. They had brought with them an impressive array of scientific equipment, which was housed in the battered shed – the Morar Village Hall of about one hundred years standing, which contained, amongst other things, shelves of ancient mildewed books. It was a strange place, and dark inside, as all the glass was broken and the windows boarded up. By comparison, the LNI site at Achnahannet was sumptuous, but it was clear the young people meant business, and for all the confusion of bedrolls scattered on the floor, and the jumble of equipment there was the unmistakable jargon of twentieth-century technology.

The LMS was out to prove or disprove that Loch Morar could support a colony of large aquatic predators, in terms of food-chain productivity – and to find out more about its monster history. The fact that it was Loch Morar and a 'Survey' meant that scientists could work quietly, away from the blaze of publicity which surrounded Loch Ness, and thus without embarrassment.

The splendid irony of the situation at Loch Ness secretly amused me, because with one of the world's greatest zoological discoveries on the brink of confirmation there was an almost total lack of scientists, zoologists in particular, who dared to join the fieldwork openly. As an engineer, I had no reputation to lose, and thus could afford to be complacent – but I did sometimes feel that British scientists were behaving with mouse-like timidity, ready to scuttle for cover at the slightest sign of risk to their precious reputations and sense of respectability. With rare exceptions, they did nothing to help – indeed the most damning criticism one could make was to say they did nothing. But there were a few exceptions and most of those who became involved in the search were honest, and open and sincere about it; and they worked hard too. The LMS was made up of them.

Moving on up the tiny loch-side single-track road, towards Bracora and the croft-house where Alan Dance had stayed the year before, we came to a small bay and inlet. Here we decided to launch *Water Horse*, leaving her swinging at anchor before proceeding to the east. The road was now so steep that I doubted if the mini and autogyro could manage it, particularly as there was a rocky outcrop and blind corner mid-way up the slope. Proceeding in the Jaguar in bottom gear, I went on to scout the way and reached the crestline without incident, Ken Wallis and the gyro chugging up behind. The view was breathtaking, far out to Brinacory Island, and then, dog-legging round the corner, Loch Morar glittered to infinity. We stopped for a little, and visited the LMS camera site and solitary attendant, perched in a tent on the very edge of a 300 ft precipice. I preferred not to think about what might happen if he sleep-walked in the night, as I had done after the *Cizara* trip.

A mile or so to the east, going downhill, we approached the croft-house which was to be our base during the week of holiday, and operations which lay ahead, and where Mrs Julie Parks came out to meet us.

My family had been at Achnahannet, and, with the exception of Simon, who had chosen to stay on expedition there, they had all come to Morar with us. It was to be something of a busman's holiday for Ken Wallis and myself, and late that same evening we motored out to look for landing places.

With the help of a farmer we chose a large field by the sea coast. It was not ideal, and had a steep downhill gradient, but as the wind would mostly blow towards it from off the sea it was usable.

Back at Bracora, we ate supper, then fell to talking with Mrs Parks about her brother's experience the year before. She was a quietly convincing person, a Scot, and her account of what had really happened confirmed the impression Alan Dance had gained of her sincerity. It had not been a laughing matter at the time; both men had been badly shaken up.

In the days that followed the West Highland coast enjoyed some lovely summer weather, and Ken Wallis flew up and down Loch Morar and over the lonely mountain peaks surrounding it. On one occasion a golden eagle approached him, giving his strange machine a very old-fashioned look before soaring away on a pair of six-foot wings. The great bird could have downed the autogyro had it collided with the rotor.

Air observation of Loch Morar, despite the crystal water, proved more difficult than at Loch Ness because of the transverse ripple effect caused by the wind blowing across the loch instead of up and down it; and although Ken put in many hours of work and even flew a sortie to Loch Shiel nearby, which historically had monster-evidence, no new sightings were recorded. As we had installed a 40-horsepower engine on little *Water Horse* for the first time I was able to operate at speed, and use her as a target for the autogyro.

The small boat now moved across the water with the grace and speed of a hydroplane cleaving the glassy surface in a shimmering cascade of ripples. I was new to it and would stand at the wheel in the cockpit and skim the craft across the vast, empty, dreamlike pools of Loch Morar, the wind streaming through my hair, as I banked and turned in a form of water ballet. It was an ecstatic experience, but from a practical viewpoint *Water Horse* made a useful aiming point for Wallis, his frame-mounted gun cameras shooting long bursts of movie film, as he zoomed and hurtled across our wake; this resulted in some of the most dramatically clear and colourful low-level 'shoot-up' film imaginable.

My family took part in it, enjoying every minute, and when the time came for us to leave Loch Morar we did so reluctantly. It had proved to be another experience for them as new and different as the journey in *Cizara*, and when we returned to Achnahannet, burnt brown by the sun, we found a disgruntled team of watchers. For some reason the Great Glen had stubbornly remained obscured by rain and mist throughout the whole period.

The balance of the year at Loch Ness was taken up with more experiments – sonars, baits, sonic devices, hydrophones, and infra-red photography, each attended by groups of specialists who added something to the pattern and colour of events. Bob Love's 'under-water people' at Urquhart Bay were again active and although they were not to return to the Ness during the three years that followed (1971–4), the expeditions and expeditioners continued to increase like waves upon the shore.

There would be long periods of calm, the off-seasons when ideas

K

would originate and build up in a surge of human interest, coming to their peak in a flurry of excitement, only to collapse inevitably in turmoil.

In watching them it was possible to stand aside, in thought, to measure each successive ripple as it built up – wondering how far it would advance before it too had spent its human energy, that marvellous, irrepressible dynamic force.

At the end of every major expedition, when this force had been most powerful, where the collective magnetism of different personalities could be felt, the collapse and withdrawal of it was hard to bear. There would be moments of emptiness, of sadness, made more poignant by the unexpected quiet.

Achnahannet, with all its long history of effort, of successes and of failures, was always vibrant with sound: human voices, laughter, the crunch of gravel, motor exhausts, songs, music, the clatter of utensils, the foreign dialogue. It had been a place of movement, and colour and variety, and when in 1973 a further extension of planning permission for it could no longer be obtained, it was finally closed down – its battered caravans removed.

In place of it today the cattle graze, peacefully munching shoots of grass, sprouting up through rubble where once a hundred thousand footsteps trod.

> The olden Sun beyond the Hills
>   Sinks, the old Winds blow
>   The same old splendid passion thrills
> The same new Splendours glow
>   Look back, and it may be that you
>   Find Life and Love and Joy anew
> Once they were ours! They shall return
> The same old fires anew shall burn

I do not know who wrote these words of poetry, but in them may be found the source, the very essence of the life force which makes all human endeavour worthwhile; and the true measure of success.

14
The underwater people

All the monster-hunting people, as well as their activities, tended to fall into categories. These in turn were determined by particular human or technological interests. For example, there were the surface photographers who monitored the vast mysterious reaches of water with their long lenses; who enjoyed the 'photographic process', and who had an eye for composition and the stunning grandeur of the scenery.

There were of course the air photographers and the underwater photographers too – the latter breed becoming a part of another separate group which, by virtue of its size and varied interests, might be described as the 'underwater people'. This group included the submariners, the divers, the marine archaeologists, scientific researchers, sonar and acoustic experts, the harbour builders (or wet-suit slaves) and to some extent the police, although the latter only operated when crashed vehicles plummeted into the loch by accident, or when suicides jumped in quite voluntarily.

In one way or another all these people had an interest in the monstrous three-dimensional underwater kingdom contained by the walls of Loch Ness, which was until recently a secret place scarcely explored and incorrectly mapped. In 1969, *Pisces* had found the loch to be much deeper than suspected, and with the introduction of search-sonars, for the first time accurate, detailed topography began to come up on the charts.

With the exception of rare contacts made by trawler fish-finders, which had been left on during transit, the Monster avoided acoustic detection until 1960, and again in 1962 when the Oxford and Cambridge joint undergraduates' expedition recorded strong echoes coming from large moving and diving objects, which did not appear to be fish. It was then not until 1968 that Professor D. Gordon

Tucker's results for Birmingham University re-awakened interest in sonars as a tool, confirmed by Bob Love's mobile sonar 'blips' from *Rangitea* in 1969; the year in which the Americans had set foot on the Moon. In 1970 it was the Americans who scored another success at Loch Ness with a truly definitive sonar.

In September three members of the Academy of Applied Science from Belmont, Massachusetts, appeared. They brought with them a new type of side-scan sonar designed and manufactured by one of the party, Dr Martin Klein. Dr Robert Rines, president of the Academy, and Mr Isaac S. Blonder, chairman of the board of the Blonder Tongue Laboratories made up the balance of the team. They were both versed in physics and electronics engineering.

The side-scan transducer was attached to scaffolding off a small pier in Urquhart Bay, and late one evening, only a short time after installation, the chart recorder picked up large intruding echoes moving through the sonar screen. Coincidentally, at this point two divers who were working on the wreck of an old craft discovered by Bob Love's team the year before lost contact with the hull down in the inky blackness of water. Ascending with arms linked, all four of their flippered feet touched something simultaneously. Reaching the surface and the awaiting boat, both men rapidly climbed out of the water – and, ashore, when comparing notes and their watches, one of which had been stopped deliberately at that moment, it became obvious that their physical contact and the sonar contact had occurred together.

The divers suggested it could have been the mast of the sunken ship, leaning out at an angle, but at their request, next day, the Academy's bait bag moored nearby was removed. It contained hormones, and other exotic substances which were known to attract aquatic animals.

Following this strange and unnerving experience, the sonar transducer, or 'towfish', and the recording equipment was put aboard *Water Horse*, and moved down to Fort Augustus 18 miles away, to troll the south-west shoreline.

After weeks of bad weather Loch Ness was again calm, and without the clutter of echoes from the surface waves the sonar chart was free of interference. We left the Abbey Haven and with Marty

Klein making the adjustments inside the cabin, Bob Rines and I slipped the yellow towfish, and watched it stabilize underwater, trailed by a thick electric cable. We lowered away until it was down a couple of hundred feet, and well astern before setting a parallel course to shore, at barely 2 knots.

Figure 9   Trailing the towfish

The plan was simple enough; we would stand off at an approximately constant distance, and allow the two fan beams to feel out the loch walls underwater on one side, and the cavernous depths on the other. Echoes coming back were picked up by the transducer, and fed through a maze of electronics to come up on the chart as sepia shadings.

The chart machine produced a double-sided picture, much like an inky signature folded over; and when in operation the paper undulated, wiped by a revolving contact helix, burning it slightly, and thus producing the varying depths of sepia shading.

I was not an electronics man or a member of the underwater people, in the sense that I was not a diver or a technical expert in the field, and although I had seen much of their operations in 1969, it was always at a distance. But now things were different, and I watched fascinated as Marty twiddled knobs and hummed a little ditty. He was entirely relaxed, sitting in the cabin, and obviously knew exactly what adjustments to make.

Scouting the shoreline, lonely and beautiful, we passed the Glendoe burn, then the rocky granite bluffs beneath 'Corrie's Cave' once the hiding place of a Highland chieftain.

Early in the year a party had set out from Achnahannet to investigate the place. Corrie's Cave was an awesome split in the mountainside, a diagonal crevasse, dripping with moisture, and perched on the edge of a precipice. It had taken a morning's hike to get there, and with the help of a rope a fearless Australian who was then at the LNI, plunged into the abyss. The cleft dropped into the blackness beyond the ledge on which I stood with a torch flaming and sputtering. Down below I could just make out the clawlike white of a hand grasping a boulder for support. The Australian returned, having satisfied himself there was no point in going on – to my infinite relief. Slightly claustrophobic, I could not see myself as a potential rescuer.

Corrie's Cave was no place for the timid, but as nature had hidden it so well the risks to be enjoyed there would probably never claim a victim; because no one could find it without the help of a guide. The chieftain had lived there without detection, though how he concealed the smoke from fires is difficult to understand.

Down below, in *Water Horse*, fish were coming up on the sonar chart as dots, tiny specks, and the loch walls and bottom silt as artistic scrolls of shading – indeed it was visually so pleasing that Marty told me a chart had once been put on show at an art exhibition.

Further along, opposite a series of five headlands the bottom receded on the chart. High above us a pyramid of stone pointed a finger to the sky – the Hambro Memorial, built there in the early 1930s in memory of Mrs Olaf Hambro who lost her life off-shore at this point in mysterious circumstances. I knew of the story, and had heard a dozen variations, some exaggerated. But I also knew an elderly Highlander, one of whose relatives was in service at Glendoe Lodge at the time when the Hambros were in residence. The true account involved a motorboat, and a fire aboard. The Hambros, two children and their nanny were left drifting in the blazing craft. Mr Hambro swam ashore with one of the children, closely followed by his wife, who was a famous golfer of the time and a powerful swimmer. There was no great distance to swim, but the water was icy cold and immensely deep. Mrs Hambro just disappeared, suddenly and without sound or splashing. Her body was never recovered. Divers went down, but found nothing in the blackness. They returned unnerved, vowing not to enter the water again.

R. T. Gould, in his famous and original book *The Loch Ness Monster and Others*, referred to this incident:

A tragic fatality in 1932 directed attention to two associated myths of the many connected with the Loch; that it 'never gives up its dead', and that its sides are honeycombed, below water, with enormous caverns. The first of these is simply untrue – and there is no evidence worthy of the name to support the second. Several bodies have been washed ashore in Loch Ness. . . . And while divers have been credited, in the Press, with seeing caverns, I suspect that such reports emanated from persons who knew very little about diving.

Gould's critical remarks prove that where Loch Ness is concerned it is best not to be too sure about anything, because as we proceeded with the sonar, the chart recorded markings which, for the first time, proved that there *were* long ridges and undercuts beneath the surface. Furthermore, apropos of divers, and their often disbelieved reports, it is only fair to add that in 1969 a party of three aqualung divers plunged offshore in this region, and confirmed these cut-backs visually. On 21 May 1971 Mr J. K. Anderson of Stirling recorded the details in a letter to me:

> At a depth of about 25 feet we encountered a large boulder. We climbed around and over this – still going down. Almost immediately underneath it we saw a cut-back or overhang approximately 5–6 feet wide. Owing to bad visibility we had no idea how far this extended in either direction. We bypassed this and at a depth of about 35–40 feet saw another similar geological formation. . . . At this point in the dive we saw there was no further point in going any deeper owing to the decreasing visibility, and rather than follow the side of the loch back to the surface for fear of being trapped by an overhang, we swam due west into the loch still submerged at approximately 35 feet. At a point where we were well clear of the shelf we surfaced and swam back to the dinghy.

In two glass-calm days of work with the side-scan towfish, during which we trailed it back and forth, and sat it on the bottom on a cradle scanning the 600 ft trench beneath the Horse Shoe scree – on several occasions large, separate echo 'blips' came up on the chart. Two of these occurred roughly beneath the Hambro memorial. These blips were immensely larger than the dots produced by fish. I bore witness to them, but could not of course interpret them. This could only be attempted by someone with long experience in the sonar field.

On the third day the weather deteriorated, with the wavetops producing interference, we moved *Water Horse* back to Urquhart Bay. *En route* we passed a buoy marking one of Bob Love's hydrophone experiments which he had dotted round the loch, serviced at intervals by Ivor Newby who did the rounds in *Kelpie*. It involved a huge amount of boatwork, and much patient effort removing lids from fifty-gallon oil drums, and changing tapes inside. Ivor, who liked to move at speed, had built a peculiar raft-like contraption which he would board from *Kelpie* to do the servicing, then tow back, skipping in his wake. With an 80 horse-power engine he could travel at more than 30 knots.

Unloading the equipment at Temple Pier, the usual confusion of cables, batteries, and instruments absorbed our energies for an hour or two, and as the side-scan was booked for tests off the coast of Norway we had to say goodbye to Dr Martin Klein. I shook his hand and thanked him for 'making history', which is what in truth he had done. The Monster blips apart, no one had sonar-charted the undercuts before. This was a significant discovery.

Unfortunately, a short time afterwards, while working in the sea, the towfish we had used broke adrift and was lost. Marty returned to his home and development centre at Salem, New Hampshire, there to continue with his life's work – designing, testing and manufacturing electronic tools for underwater exploration. He was an acknowledged world authority on sonars, and a brilliant innovator.

On his departure, I drove *Water Horse* back to the Horse Shoe scree, with Bob Rines, Ike Blonder, and Rip Hepple aboard, towing the *Moo-scow* dinghy loaded with equipment. Ike had borrowed a tape recorder for use with hydrophones, and we had the sex-lures aboard and tubs of other attractants, with which we hoped to interest the Beast. It was a lighthearted trip with the two Americans quipping back and forth, and the Englishmen saying little; contrasting national habits, which blended well together. Arriving late, with the great wall of the Horse Shoe scree above us, Ike lowered the hydrophone in 600 feet of water; on the way down it struck something solid, scraping over it, producing loud rasping noises through the speaker on the boat – before going down unhindered another 200 feet.

We were right in the place of a major sonar contact. Later the hydrophone picked up underwater pulses of sound, which were recorded on the tape. We buoyed the sex attractants, and spread the salmon oils, wondering what would happen if the animal surfaced beneath us. It was an eerie experience, and when the light had all but gone we journeyed back to Fort Augustus, trailing Rip Hepple in the *Moo-scow* dinghy, reeking of salmon oils. He had accidentally slipped and fallen into a pool of it lying in the boat.

Ike Blonder returned to America, and for a day or two Bob Rines and I continued the pursuit, playing eel noises out through a speaker underwater. These were strange cheeping noises repeated over and over. We left Abbey Haven early each morning, with the sunrise painting the clouds above the mountain tops – a surrealist world, and a time during which a friendship developed between us.

Bob Rines had first become intrigued by the mystery when reading Constance Whyte, as I had done myself in 1959. Her book *More Than a Legend* nurtured an interest which changed both our lives.

Before his departure that autumn we flew down to London at the LNI's request to attend a press conference on the side-scan results. Dr Rines spoke clearly about the potential meaning of these, but pointed out the difficulties experienced with all sonar systems. He promised the Academy would publish a statement when Klein's analysis was complete; and later Klein Associates produced a report on the whole episode, with photos and charts included in it.

It was a fittingly reserved account, balancing the facts of the results against the difficulty of interpretation:

In summary our brief side-scan sonar tests in Loch Ness in 1970 produced three important discoveries.
1 There are large moving objects in the Loch.
2 There is abundant fish life in the loch which could support a large creature.
3 There are large ridges in the steep walls of the Loch which could conceivably harbor large creatures.
Despite our relative success in our experiments, we find our ability to make conclusive statements limited by the state of the art in underwater search equipment. Much has been written about the ultra high resolution systems and three dimensional systems utilizing imaging techniques and acoustic holography. At this point, however, these systems tend to be laboratory curiosities which are not yet available, to the author's knowledge,

in commercially practical realizations. Neither the English, who have done so much of the pioneering work in sonar, nor the Americans are yet able to produce a system which can conclusively prove or disprove the old controversy of the mysterious monster.

These balanced words probably did more for credibility than a pageful of rhetoric. Marty Klein knew his stuff, and also its limitations; but of one thing he was entirely certain – the 'large ridges' and the undercuts:

Our records revealed some of the spectacular geology of the steep walls of the Loch . . . [see Plate 21] . . . Note that the long dark sections are apparently highly reflective ridges while the long light sections are areas where there is a depression or undercut which gives no signal return. Unfortunately, we cannot determine actual depth of these depressions, but they appear to be certainly wide enough to harbor large animal life. Some of my colleagues have kindly suggested that these structures be named the 'Klein Caves' of Loch Ness. We hope to return with a narrow conical beam sonar to look straight in at the walls to determine the actual depth of these undercuts.

Inevitably, with the season's close in 1970 the underwater people departed from the loch. Bob Love's contingent at Temple Pier, with all its activity: its diving teams and archaeologists working on the wreck (possibly a *Zulu* bluff-hulled sailing craft built 100 years before), its hydrophone listening sets and other devices were brought ashore.

The job of analysing results would take months to complete, and one result in particular was causing interest. Strange, almost synchronous, rhythms of 'clicks' had been recorded on tape, for which there seemed to be no ready explanation.

The digital fixed-beam sonar used by the Birmingham University team had not made any new contacts, and the brief but colourful 'Black & White' Scotch-sponsored expedition from America had not come up with anything apart from the diver's momentary brush with something underwater.

I had for long been concerned about the safety of divers in Loch Ness, but recognized the futility of getting them to take the Monster seriously. As none of them had seen it, they pretended not to be deterred by it, or by the possibility of attack. Most underwater people were absorbed by the environment – in the same way that in my youth I had been absorbed by the 'realm of the aviator', the boundless oceans of the air above.

Again, in 1971, the underwater people were back in operation in both Loch Morar and Loch Ness, although the tools they used were monitored from the surface. By now the Loch Morar Survey had grown in complexity, and after a successful news-conference and the publication of a report they were fielding a bigger team, with three isolated camera stations, and a bottom-sampling programme to add to the information needed to assess the biology and geology of the loch.

Having taken another busman's holiday from the fieldwork at Loch Ness, I launched *Water Horse* on Loch Morar, and spent a blissful week living aboard her at night, dividing my time between exploration, helping the LMS supply their outposts, and the Academy underwater people who came in briefly.

Ike Blonder and his elder son Greg appeared first with a mass of hydrophone equipment: a stereophonic hydrophone set, and a most ingenious listening/playback device developed at the Blonder Tongue Laboratories in New Jersey. It consisted of a hydrophone which recorded incoming sounds, then played them back moments later underwater. The idea was to excite the curiosity of an approaching animal by making it talk back to itself, in effect, should it be capable of making sounds or should it use a sonar of its own. The pulses of sound recorded in the Horse Shoe trench the year before had shown a definite pattern when photographed on a TV tube. The shape indicated a possible animal sonar. The idea had been tried before, with birds, and it had caused them to become very much excited.

With the watchful approach of the LMS, who came alongside in a boat, the first tests with the stereophonic hydrophones proved interesting. Listening through headphones one could pick up the sound of outboard motors 4 or 5 miles distant. There was a ringing clarity about it, but apart from that – nothing; then technical problems began to develop, which put the equipment out of use. It was very frustrating.

For two days we did our best, in blustery, sunny weather, *Water Horse* rolling badly, but without effect. Gremlins had got into the instruments, and as Ike succumbed to sea-sickness, we had to call a halt. He went back to Loch Ness, and his place was taken by Bob Rines who brought with him a strange new set of equipment – a synchronous strobe-light underwater movie camera.

This ingenious instrument was housed in a pair of pressure-resistant cylinders, and could be left moored underwater for long periods, taking flashlight pictures at set intervals. Rines had first tried it out at Achnahannet, where he had imported it through a somewhat puzzled British Customs, and after functional tests the need arose for calibration in clear water. The only solution was to borrow the municipal swimming baths at Inverness, which was arranged, though with the proviso that we finished work by 9 a.m.! But as the LNI's mobile cameras were out at 5.30 a.m. we had time to fit it in, and to use the first batch of school children who came to the baths as swimming targets.

The time for operations in the loch had now arrived, and with much careful thought and preparation the equipment was anchored to the bottom near the mouth of the river Coiltie, with three buoys attached, and yards of slack in the line. This was a good place for night-time monster visitors, and as far as we knew, comparatively shallow.

Next morning, there was no sign of the equipment, or the marker buoys which should have remained afloat even if the strobe had been pulled into deeper water.

It was a blow. The device had been prepared at the Massachusetts Institute of Technology, by Professor Harold Edgerton, inventor of the strobe, and pioneer in underwater time-lapse photography. We wondered what had happened to it. Binocular searches of the loch in all directions produced nothing, and inquiries round about were equally fruitless, although I had my doubts about the local salmon poachers, who always worked at night. In 1969 I had seen enough of them from *Water Horse*, moving about in rowing boats. One could always tell a poacher at night because the oar strokes were twice as fast as normal. They fished the river mouths in Urquhart Bay – and they resented intruders.

On the off-chance of spotting the equipment still flashing underwater, I made contact with two professional divers, who came over hurriedly from Inverness and plunged for us. We could see the mushroom bubbles marking progress, but they had to work by feel in the darkness along a steep underwater slope, which went down to over 100 ft, in a tangle of sunken logs and branches. We called a halt, and pulled the two men back on board. There was no point in risking lives.

The loss of this equipment was a disaster, but when we had given up all hope of it, returning to Achnahannet by road to eat an evening meal, *Fussy Hen* was sighted coming round the point half a mile away, and was seen to stop, and the helmsman pull something up from the water.

On getting closer, incredibly, it was seen to be the strobe set, unharmed and still functioning. Rip Hepple on board the boat had simply noticed the buoys as he motored past, and stopped to investigate. How the equipment had drifted two miles against the wind into the main loch was difficult to understand. Subsequent development of the film showed nothing but water, and in one or two frames loops of sisal rope. Logically, it must have been the poachers who had towed the equipment away and dumped it – and as Hepple later pointed out, the sea-anchor effect of the camera equipment underwater could have moved it with a current, overcoming the wind-drift of the floats.

But whatever the explanation, the recovery of this equipment was to have a crucial effect on future operations, and in 1971, the results obtained with it were interesting. Clear colour pictures taken in Loch Morar showing rocks and the bottom topography up to a range of 60 ft; whereas in Loch Ness, salmon could be seen at 15 ft or so. Beyond, objects became indistinct due to the peat content of the water. Amongst other puzzling results, curious 'winged' creatures an inch or two in length, were repeatedly photographed at depths of 50 ft, which looked like aquatic bumble-bees. Crustacea perhaps, or larvae of some kind, they proved a source of speculation. Another photograph showed the possible remains of a 'Nessie' carcass lying on the bottom, complete with long neck and head. This could have been a tree trunk or a ridge of silt, but for two small objects in the picture which looked suspiciously like bones.

Currents in Loch Ness, and in particular Urquhart Bay, had never been studied in any great depth, and the bottom topography could affect them. Bob Rines spent many hours criss-crossing the bay monitoring a small echo-chart recorder, which we had used in Morar to help the LMS with their bottom-sampling programme. As a result of this work he was to build an impressive three-dimensional model of Urquhart Bay, expanded three times vertically, to accentuate the spectacular troughs and ridges which he plotted with the sonar.

Unfortunately, the exploration was limited to Urquhart Bay because of the untimely death of a man who had planned to map the whole loch in this way. Major Eustace Maxwell had been active at Loch Ness in his boat *Black Pearl*, which he had rigged with echo sounders. Eustace was the brother of a famous Monster witness, the late Gavin Maxwell, author of *Ring of Bright Water*, whom I had met a few years previously in London through another odd coincidence. The illustrator for his book, Robin McEwan (who produced the marvellous otter pictures) was then acting as 'QC' for the defence in television's 'Your Witness' series, in which the Monster evidence was tried before a panel of jurors.

At Achnahannet, Eustace Maxwell frequently called in to discuss his plans; but as he died of a coronary in the winter of 1970, his grandiose scheme never came to fruition.

Another Loch Ness project was at this time being carried out by Dr Steve Thorpe and his team from the National Institute of Oceanography (NIO). For two years they had been working on a study of the phenomenon known as a 'seiche', and were able to prove it existed, on the basis of temperature measurements and movements of the thermocline.

To put it simply, a seiche is an internal wave, or disturbance of water in a lake between two thermal and density layers, and can best be demonstrated by the filling of a long glass tube with two differently-coloured fluids, which do not mix. When tilting the tube, an internal wave can be seen to travel down the tube, and back again in oscillation.

On a giant scale this is what happened in Loch Ness, only the period of oscillation was found to be fifty-six hours, and the amplitude or height of the wave underwater was almost a hundred feet. It was a slow-motion effect with no visible result on the surface, which changed level by no more than half an inch.

In making these tests and observations the NIO people became a familiar part of the scene, with their boats and equipment, and for a time they worked from below Achnahannet, making use of the harbour there.

On 2 September 1971, Dr Thorpe read a paper before the British Association for the Advancement of Science, under the title 'A Model for C.A.T. and the Monster Internal Waves of Loch Ness'. This was at once pounced upon by the press, and misconstrued, as it ignored the fact that within the report Steve Thorpe had said: 'There is no relation that I can see between the internal seiche and any animate monster in Loch Ness.'

Press coverage of all kinds and standards could be met with at Loch Ness. Some of it was good, with intelligent reporting, and some of it was execrable. The majority of journalists were polite and reasonable, and a few were unmitigated pests.

It was the policy of the LNI and all serious independents to help the press, and to release news items to them as fairly as possible. This was not an easy thing to do as newspapers are very much in competition, and a 'first come first served' principle is expected. However, with one notable exception, peace was maintained. On this one occasion I was rung up and questioned about a visiting Swiss inventor, who claimed to have an electronic device which had an effect on certain mammals, causing them to become disorientated. He wanted to try it underwater in Loch Ness. The lower power of this device, barely 60 watts, indicated to me that it could not injure anything electrically, and it seemed only sporting to help him from a boat – but without the glare of publicity. For saying 'no' to one member of the press I was treated to an ugly flow of invective over the telephone – an extraordinary outburst, which I would have done well to record for the Press Association to hear.

As it was, the experiments were done without interference and apparently without effect; but then I never did think the Monster was a mammal. The Swiss inventor proved to be a man of charm and brilliance, and it was a pleasure to work with him during the course of his experiments.

As a photographer, I found the underwater people and their experiments a constant source of entertainment. Divers and submarines are photogenic subjects, and even electronic equipment has a certain pictorial quality. I shot many hundreds of feet of colour film of these activities for the historical record, which was slowly building up; and working so closely with them it was inevitable I should try an experiment myself, using an underwater speaker, to which I rigged a tape recorder.

It had been known for many years that music attracts animals – or perhaps one should say that some music attracts some animals. For example waltz rhythms are known to attract fish, which swim round the source in enormous barrel-like shoals. Cows too are seen to cross a field and approach the source of melodic, peaceful music.

Experimenting, I found the glass hull of *Water Horse* acted like a sounding board, so that when I sat in the cabin the flood of music underwater could be heard mysteriously. The occupants of fishing boats would react to this. I could see the men looking round, wondering where the lovely sound was coming from – the cadences of Beethoven's Pastoral Symphony echoing underwater. Of all the unsuccessful experiments, I enjoyed it the most!

During the Loch Ness Investigation of 1971 an experiment was tried with fish-finding sonars, which had a real potential, but it, too, was a disappointment. I had made arrangements through the Caledonian Canal authorities to approach the trawler skippers in transit through the loch. At the point of entry the lock keeper would hand over a letter, asking for the fish-finder to be left on – and for the skipper to submit the chart on exit, in return for a nominal sum in payment.

L

It was a good idea, and we hoped to collect a hundred end-to-end charts in this way; and perhaps some statistics.

Unfortunately, the majority of skippers just didn't co-operate, and the few who did generally put the chart machine on 'slow', with the result that twenty-four miles of loch was shrunk up to as many inches on the paper, which made it difficult to read.

In spite of these setbacks however, about a quarter of the twenty charts had something noted on them – some echo response which made the skipper curious. It was a beginning, and with the dawning of 'respectability' we felt that trawler skippers in the future might voluntarily come to assist the underwater people.

15
TV, talks
and travels

O' Nessie, just whoar med thoo be
Won't thoo cum oot in't oppen?
We're maist purplexed, wad like tae see
Just whoar aboots thoo's stoppen
A Blessin' on thee scaly hide,
That's if thee hide be scaly,
We've chessed an' huntid far an' wide
For thee, Beeath neet an' daily

Sum fwoak'll say they've hed a gliff
O thee, if just fur t'minnet,
Bit ah'll believe seck gossep, if
T'war nowt bit trewth 'at's in it:
An' yit, yan knaws wat sum'll say
Tae cause a greet norayshun:
If thoo finnds time tae pop ooar way,
Git oot at Carlisle Stayshun

by Derwent Pickering who 'sharpened his dialect quill' after a talk
given by the author at Whitehaven, in West Cumberland.

Since the introduction of television on a national and then an
international scale through satellites, the 'media', as they have come
to be known, have revolutionized world communications. Today
we are in contact with events as they happen, everywhere, and this
leads to a degree of internationalism which was impossible a few
years ago; and as TV consumes so much information, there is always
space for new programmes on controversial subjects. Television
thrives on controversy.

In the years following the 'Panorama' programme in 1960 with Richard Dimbleby, I became involved in other TV productions, each of which was in some way connected with the Monster. Cliff Michelmore's '24 Hours' and 'Tonight' programmes, Eamonn Andrews's 'Today' programme, Ludovic Kennedy's 'Your Witness', Hughie Green's 'The Sky's the Limit', the children's 'Summerhouse' and 'Blue Peter' programmes, BBC and ITV News, and the regional companies all 'had a go' at one time or another, and I must admit I enjoyed these excursions. Television has a quality of its own, a form of excitement, a nerve-wracking anticipation which is fun and which brings an interview to life. Live shows always have the edge on taped shows for this reason.

Not all of these interviews were lighthearted, and I would sometimes find that personalities who were friendly before the show would attack me fiercely once it had started. There was nothing underhand in this – they wanted to get the most out of the controversy. On only one occasion was I treated badly, but that was before the show began. I knew my questioner had not done his homework, and during the rehearsal sparks flew between us; but he was an honest person, and after the row did his best for the subject when the programme went out live.

By comparison, radio interviews were more relaxed, the tapes could be cut and juggled to suit the mood; but again, there was something distinctive about them. Pure sound has its advocates, and with so much television there has been a resurgence in radio, and the numbers who listen to it.

The strangest radio interview I had was in 1971 at Inverness: moments after seeing the Monster's head and neck from *Water Horse* I had switched on a tape recorder to make a commentary, and BBC radio wanted to use it for a science programme. I was told to go to Inverness, to a do-it-yourself studio where I would find instructions awaiting me. Arriving there I found the place deserted and no instructions either! With only half an hour in which to sort out the problem, and faced with a battery of switches, microphones, and warning lights, it seemed insurmountable. Searching, I found an engineer's specification for the whole studio layout, and frantically leafed through it hoping to pinpoint useful data.

Gradually I was able to cut in power, lights and microphones; but I could go no further than that. I could not raise the London Studio. In desperation, I rang the BBC at Glasgow, to ask for help, and they phoned engineers at Aberdeen. They did not know the layout either, but after much switching and experimenting London came in on the speaker, perhaps two minutes before the programme time. It was a peculiar experience, sitting in the studio, chatting to the interviewer and playing my own tape to him through a maze of electronics, with absolutely no one else about. Studios are normally full of technicians, directors and organizers, all of whom concentrate on getting the programme out. After an experience like that I felt that nothing was impossible; and it proved the old adage that when in doubt 'press on'.

On the lecture front too, I had some odd experiences, some of which were hilariously funny, and some not. By 1973 I had talked informally, and lectured to a great many audiences in the United Kingdom, to most of the universities, and to countless societies, clubs and institutes. I had been on tours to both coasts of the USA, and on visits to Scandinavia and Europe. There was no end to these activities, but due to the marathon nature of the hunt, there was time for them. Fourteen annual 'off seasons' provided scope.

The funniest events usually occurred at universities, where no one was ever sure who was coming, or how large the audience would be – or if indeed there would be an audience. The smallest university audience, because of some mix-up in the planning, was about six, and the largest over a thousand. Once, due to the continuing influx of students we had to move from one lecture hall to a bigger one, because there was so much pushing and shouting by the multitudes left outside that the organizers feared a riot. Once at a Cambridge University literary meeting, the projector was so blurred we had to stop to investigate. Because of the mass of young folk sitting round in damp clothing (after walking through the rain) steam had arisen in clouds to fog the condensers!

In California, at a university talk, no one knew for sure how to work the lecture theatre, a superb modern place with a forest of controls. When the time came to project a film, switches were pulled, and the screen rolled itself up to hide in the ceiling. More switches brought unwanted light effects, and the movement of stage furniture. The audience went into hysterics.

Occasions on which films stuck and burned in the gate, and when slides came in upside down were commonplace, but people were always ready to laugh. Sometimes, during the course of a lecture there would be such gales of laughter that I began to feel uncomfortable; to look behind to see if my shirt tail was hanging out. With more experience, I could judge an audience. Some were very serious, and some quick-witted. Others were stonily dumb. Amongst the brightest were the school audiences, with a freshness and originality at question time – and amongst the dullest, the 'senior' audiences, the older qualified folk who seemed afraid to speak or make a fool of themselves. Sadly, accomplishment can have a shrouding effect once people become aware of it.

Perhaps the most obvious lesson to come out of the lecturing experience was that human beings are petrified of ridicule – or the fear of ridicule. The more important the person, the more loth he would be to risk it. This led to what I would refer to as the 'ho ho ho' introductions. People who were fascinated by the Monster, and who really knew a lot about it, and who had invited me to speak would, at the last minute, funk the introduction. They would say something which put them safely on the fence, and me on the wrong side of it.

In extreme cases, as an insurance against a 'failed lecturer', after-dinner speakers would have something else funny to say, but this type of prepared cleverness, or histrionic hindsight failed dismally. It was all very human, and understandable, and as the Monster evidence *was* so incredible, no blame attached to anyone. The important thing was to be allowed to present it sensibly, and for this I owed a debt of thanks to all these people.

Film making at Loch Ness, apart from the miles of footage shot by amateurs, was invariably for TV commentaries, or interviews, or mystery series, and documentaries. The film was shot on 16mm stock, and on 35mm for the cinema and the more important TV epics, like the Disney film made in 1969 which was animated, costing several hundred thousand dollars.

Film-making teams would visit briefly, and at the LNI, Italian and Norwegian TV crews made documentaries. The crews reflected national character, and were highly entertaining. One crew was international and included two Greeks, a Cockney, an Italian lady organizer of great charm called Gabriella Pescatore, and others who were nicknamed for convenience, 'icecremo', 'mafioso' and the like, because no one could pronounce their real names properly.

Nicknames were commonplace at the LNI, and no one took offence at them. They tended to be based on appearance, habit or character, or sometimes no good reason whatsoever. 'Tombstone', 'Squizz', 'Bear', 'Mountain Man', 'Dave' 1, 2, 3, 4, etc., all the way up to 8, and so forth. The ladies more often retained their Christian names, but there were a few exceptions.

In 1971 the Norwegian TV people arrived to make a film for a mystery series and proceeded to work with good-humoured competence. They were a close-knit team, obviously Scandinavian, spoke near perfect English and would sing songs together when travelling about. The Italians made a film for an adventure series.

All the teams were different, and some showed artistry in the filming, while others worked by numbers. Later, with the coming of small Japanese teams, I was to witness a different approach. They were not so much interested in the Monster as in the scenery and the atmosphere of mystery. They would react instantly, to film sudden natural effects of light and shade, whereas some of the other professionals would spend hours on a few set pieces.

Once, in Urquhart Bay, a cinema team hired local boatmen to make artificial mist – smoke billowing out from canisters; and ignored the marvellous natural mist effects which developed in the early morning.

Due to the grandeur of the scenery, and in places its uniqueness, other film makers began to appear at Loch Ness. In 1971 a TV series was shot in Glen Affric nearby – which rang to musket shots, and whoops from Indians. In 1973 'The Pathfinders' was filmed there, in which a small army of Redcoats appeared, and a hundred-year-old sailing ship.

I had watched parts of the filming, and had been intrigued by the infectious dramatism, which is the essence of the 'motion picture industry'. In 'The Pathfinders' I became a Redcoat for one day's work as an extra, charging up and down the mountainside in Glen

Affric shouting hoarsely, and firing blanks through a musket. It was colourful, but exhausting, and with a forest of real 2 ft bayonets at one's back in a charge, extremely dangerous. One got the impression that 'extras' were expendable.

Watching the ancient and lovely sailing vessel - a barquentine – from the waters of Urquhart Bay, and the Indians and Redcoats all fighting each other and falling overboard from the rigging, I shot more 16mm film in colour for the ever-expanding Loch Ness records. Again it had nothing to do with monster-hunting, but their antics had become a part of history.

Each of these episodes covered a small part of the season's work, and variations which were as numerous as those in a kaleidoscope.

After the Norwegian TV people came to Loch Ness I was invited to Oslo in late December, to take part in a discussion on television, with a zoologist from their National University. Arriving in the icy mists of early winter I passed through customs to meet their representative, who promptly lost the keys to his car in a snowdrift. After this rather mundane beginning I was dropped off at an hotel where I spent the night cat-napping under a single Scandinavian quilt, which slipped off on to the floor exposing me to the full blast of central heating. It might have been any modern glass-and-concrete structure anywhere in the world – and I was grateful when a young man arrived to show me round the city, before the TV rehearsals started.

I was taken to see the magnificent Viking Ship Museum, housed in a simple church-like structure, its plain white arches beaming rays of light on to the thousand-year-old longships. One, in particular, was almost complete; and relics of footwear and clothing had been found with it, preserved in the mud. The ships were much bigger than I had expected, and I learned too that the design represented the *soe-orm*, or giant sea-snake of Norwegian legend. I knew the figurehead was based on it, but did not realize that the hull of the boat and its upswept stern were the body and tail as well. This was of great interest, as the records of the *soe-orm* off the Norwegian coast went back through the centuries, and described what could be the parental 'Nessie' species – the marine progenitor.

Close to the museum a second exhibit was on view in an entirely different setting. The *Kon Tiki* raft was displayed with all the modern trimmings, of lights, and painted scenery – models of statues from Easter Island, and a great whale-shark swimming underneath. This famous raft could not have been more artistically portrayed. The style was in contrast to the Viking ships, but it suited the present era.

Whisked away for lunch on top of a nearby range of snowclad mountains, we passed an immense artificial ski-jump. Once a year the population of Oslo would gather at this place, and cheer on the competitors. As a young man the king of Norway had won fame and the respect of his people by simply competing – and staying on his feet! At close quarters the terrifying height of this jump beggared description – the take-off platform at the top was so high it was lost to view in the mist.

The rehearsal late that afternoon took place at the ultra-modern TV centre in Oslo, and as there was time to spare afterwards, I was shown more of the city with its historic walled fort, the harbour and shipping. Next day the programme went out and although the discussion was through an interpreter, I was assured that the majority of Norwegians understood English, which explained why the film soundtrack had remained in English. I liked the blonde, active Scandinavians; and as I flew homewards over the barren frozen wastes of Oslo fjord, I wondered where the next overseas journey would take me.

In April 1972 I found out – it was to the USA again. In the spring of the preceding year the Academy of Applied Science had arranged lectures in Massachusetts and this had led to visits to New York and other interesting places. As a result a new six-weeks' tour had developed, and with this to face I arrived in New York, where the British Tourist Authority had taken up the cudgels.

It proved to be a whirlwind of appointments, interviews and rehearsals for TV, radio and the newspapers. America was fascinated by the subject of the Monster, and by showing the 1960 film, and in announcing the appearance of *Monster Hunt* which Acropolis Books of Washington, DC, had just published for me, the tour snowballed rapidly.

In New York the BTA's wonderfully efficient staff arranged four syndicated shows, 'To Tell the Truth', the 'Barry Farber Show', the 'Johnny Carson Show' and the 'Frost Show', which in turn led to local TV and radio in Boston, Washington, DC, Rochester, Detroit, and Chicago, going out through more than 550 TV and radio stations, across the USA. It was a vortex of activity and although these shows were for entertainment, I was allowed to discuss the facts, and make a case for the Monster.

While this was in progress, the first talks started, at schools and universities. At MIT an audience of perhaps 1,000 gathered and at this event at question time we had a panel of enthusiasts: Isaac Blonder, Martin Klein, Bob Rines and Professor Harold Edgerton, each of whom had contributed something special to the research, and who stood up in turn to speak.

Not all the talks were on such a scale, but on travelling to California, Bob Rines and I 'touched base' with technological groups through his network of contacts as a famous patent lawyer. In Los Angeles we talked with experts who computer-enhanced the photographs from space, and to the south at La Jolla, I spoke at the Scripps Oceanographic Institute, which is situated in one of the more attractive climate zones in America – a semi-tropical place of flowers and surfing beaches. Unhappily, there was so little time that I could not stop to enjoy it, but I did the rounds at the aquarium, and there saw the largest octopus in captivity. It reminded me of an incident at the Boston Aquarium, where an octopus of smaller size but great friendliness had tried to pull a lady zoologist into the tank. She had responded with reserve, stripping the suckered writhing tentacles from her arm while calmly asking for assistance. She was fond of the animal and told me afterwards she thought it was 'neat'.

At last we finished the appointments and as a response to all the generosity and introductions afforded me by Bob Rines of the Academy, I was glad to be able to make an introduction myself.

Ken Peterson, the Walt Disney producer, lived at Beverly Hills, and since his 1969 Loch Ness film, we had kept in touch. We met again, and he conducted us round Disneyland and the production studios at Burbank, where a rough-cut of his film was shown. Opinions varied as to how it should be treated. A comically animated

Disney Monster featured in it, together with the live interviews and the famous Loch Ness scenery. We commented on it, making a few timid suggestions, and a year later it was released on educational TV in the USA, and in Britain on cinema in 1974.

All the Disney people we met seemed to have a special character about them – and the proof of their artistry was everywhere – in the picture gallery and the drawings and sketches pinned up on the work boards – an inheritance of genius.

As a final venture we flew on to San Francisco, where Bob Rines had business and where I could relax. It was a strange place, quite unlike the city I had imagined, and in a twentieth-storey hotel room I could not help but think about the San Andreas fault, the earthquake line which runs near the city. The tall buildings were earthquake-proof – but I had my doubts about it. The truth was that after six weeks of non-stop activity across the USA I was becoming jaded, and when Bob suggested flying up to Portland in Oregon for a very special reason, my first reaction was one of homesickness – I wanted to go, but wanted to get back to my family too. I rang home across the face of half the globe to find that I had overlooked a lecture date at the Royal Radar Establishment, but the need to go to Oregon was real, and I had to cancel it.

The reason for this decision was hard to explain over the phone, but it was justifiable because of the opportunity we had to visit 'Big Foot' country.

For years I had been following the course of events and the literature concerning evidence for the huge footprints reported from the Pacific north-west of America. Ivan Sanderson the zoologist had written a 500-page book on this and allied subjects in 1961 and had sent me a copy of *Abominable Snowmen*. We had corresponded ever since, and when in New York I had visited him at his estate in the backwoods of New Jersey – at the Society for Investigating the Unexplained (SITU) which proved to be a most unusual place. Here I met an Irishman, an ex-Big Game hunter turned conservationist, called Peter Byrne. I had also seen plaster casts of a Yeti print from the Himalayas, and a 'Big Foot' print of almost human form but some 18 inches in length. They were from real prints, apparently.

Peter Byrne was now the executive director of the International

Wildlife Conservation Society (IWCS), and had just returned from eighteen months of fieldwork researching the Big Foot phenomenon. During this time had had seen fresh tracks himself, and trailed one set of them for miles.

As a result of this meeting, I had asked if Peter could speak at the Academy, which Bob Rines quickly arranged before his return to Oregon. And now we had an opportunity to visit him.

Flying over the vast terrain of northern California, with its mountains and forests, we approached the Cascade mountain range with its huge Crater Lake, evidence of a meteor strike aeons of years ago; and the snow-covered cone of Mount Hood, reaching 11,000 ft below us. It was a wild landscape, after the teeming cities of the east, and the arid deserts of central America. Landing at Portland, we motored up the Columbia river highway through towering scenery, and spent the next two days at Byrne's headquarters.

It was an experience as bizarre as my introduction to the Loch Ness Monster, and equally as real. We met and talked to an actual Big Foot witness, a schoolmaster, and taped his account. He and others had seen a gigantic fur-covered creature, standing 9 or 10 feet tall, at very close range, a mere 100 yards or so. It was upright and man-like in appearance, and strode back into the oak-forests from whence it had come, but not before the witness had viewed it through a eight-power rifle telescope, examining its features closely. It was not a spectre, or a man from outer space, and it left 20-in. footprints behind it, as witnessed by the local sheriffs who were called in to investigate. Judging by their own small footprints, which scarcely flattened the grass, the Big Foot must have weighed 600–700 pounds.

As the Big Foot had stood beneath an oaktree it was possible to gain an idea of its stature. The head had reached up to a branch. Also, its eyes had reflected car headlamps sweeping out of a driveway nearby as the vehicle turned into the road on which the witness's own car was stopped. It was dusk at the time of his sighting, and his wife was afraid, because their new baby was in the car with them. It was for this reason he had run to get his loaded rifle.

This cat-like gleam of reflected light from the creature's eyes suggested it might be nocturnal – and when checking on the branch-height I took a photograph of a 6 ft 4 in. man standing with an arm reaching above his head; to find the branch was still a foot above his finger tips!

Clearly the specimen was a male; possibly an old one because the bear-like pelt of fur was silver tipped.

Before leaving Oregon, Peter Byrne and his helper Dennis Jensen the big ex-marine who had stood below the tree, drove us out into the mountains in their 'scout' vehicle, equipped for the search and tracking operations. Altogether Byrne had put in more than 100,000 miles on searches, and in following up the clues. He had talked to some fifty witnesses of tracks and actual Big Foot sightings, and had examined sixteen sets of different tracks himself; taking a number of casts.

We drove all day, though the enormous forests, and a mountain-scape buried in snowdrifts. It was hard to imagine how any creature could survive in such a wilderness, but the fact remained that Kodiak bears survived on an island off Alaska hundreds of miles to the north, and that when reared up they stood 10 ft at the snout.

But whatever the Big Foot was, it was not a bear; and as we flew back to San Francisco, and from there across the States and the Nevada Desert – endless leagues of barren rock and dried-up watercourses – I had time to think about the problem, and the strange quirk of fate, the accident, it seemed, which had put me into the forefront of a *second* great adventure, a second hunt in pursuit of the incredible.

16
The *Hunter* expeditions

In the *New Scientist* magazine of 8 November 1973, a new term was accidentally coined by a printer's error. It appeared on the penultimate line of page 425: 'expendition'.

In all 'expenditions' there is a great expenditure of energy, time, money, resources and materials, and thus the word fits very nicely. By coincidence 'expendition' appears in an article entitled 'West Coast Scene, SASQUATCH', which is the Canadian Indian term for the Big Foot – and only one of the many native Indian terms for it. The Indians had, of course, known about it for generations, but kept quiet because their accounts were brushed aside by the white man, who knew better. Like the older local people at Loch Ness who had seen the Monster, silence proved to be the most convenient policy.

In the article reference is made to the latest book by John Green, 'a small town journalist in British Columbia' (in fact an editor of a newspaper, who has spent many years researching the phenomenon at first hand), in which he lists some 500 of the 800 sightings he has on record:

> The file is naturally incomplete because, as Green states, most people would question the sanity of anyone reporting such an encounter. Grover Kranz, an anthropologist of Washington State University and one of the few professionals on the Sasquatch trail, states that probably ten times as many persons encounter Sasquatch as deign to mention it.

Sighting numbers of this order are interesting because they begin to compare with those from Loch Ness, and in the case of the Big Foot also, the closer one gets to the mystery the more real it becomes.

This is the hall-mark of fact – and in consequence the need to get as close as possible to a living specimen becomes important. I was very much aware of this, and in the spring of 1971 Jim Ewing, the Scot I knew in Reading, suggested to me that a bigger boat on Loch Ness would prove an advantage, because *Water Horse* was too small for comfort, and was not designed for rough conditions. She was potentially very fast and easy to handle, but I had found that big waves slowed her down. This meant that on long journeys on the Ness, if it was rough, I had to stand at the wheel for hours. Blasting through under power caused such buffeting, I was afraid of splitting the hull.

I was much attached to the little craft, but when Jim showed me the new hull he had in mind, a Fairey-Hunt 18, designed for offshore work, I capitulated.

Water Horse was pensioned off, and the new boat which we named *Hunter* was built up during the winter to our own specification. She was spartan, a work-boat in every sense, but with a big cockpit and a deep-vee hull in fibreglass, she was immensely strong. When on the water with a 50 horse-power outboard and 'thunderbolt' ignition she had both speed and reliability. *Hunter* was a beaut.

We first launched on the Thames at Caversham, and motored sedately upstream. It was no test of performance, but the craft took the water evenly. It was not until mid-July of 1972 that I towed her the 600 miles north, to keep a film-making date with an English camera man, on contract to the Japanese. The weather had been appalling, with rain and winds blotting out the spring and early summer. Sleeping in the boat parked in a mountain lay-by chilled me to the bone, but as had happened before, on arriving at Dalcross airport to collect the camera man, the sun came out. We travelled to Loch Ness, where he got his pictures in almost tropical conditions.

This cheered him up, and I waved goodbye before setting off for Loch Morar, where the LMS was gathering for its third and final summer's work. I was now on the committee, and knew that it would be a major undertaking. The LMS had been given a large sum of money by an anonymous donor, who was impressed by its work and *The Search for Morag*, the book they had just published on their findings. They had uncovered historical information and many new sightings; and a sum total of biological facts which proved the loch was able to support a colony of predators. It was a good start, and hopes were high.

Towing *Hunter* along the miles of single track, around blind corners and up near-vertical gradients was a nerve-wracking experience. Occasional fish lorries packed with tons of smelly herring scraped by with inches to space. It was a long journey, and when the ancient corrugated Morar shed hove into view I pulled up with relief. The LMS team appeared in stages, towing caravans and other impedimenta. We decided to camp in the field that night, then push on to find a base camp further down the loch.

Next day, White Beach was chosen, a low lying patch of shingle barely accessible to motor vehicles. To get there meant driving down a narrow track which threatened to tip one into the loch, but it had the advantage of checking all but the most intrepid.

We launched the boat at the inlet where *Water Horse* had first been slipped, and when my kit was aboard I set course for White Beach, some 2 miles eastward of the islands. As I opened the throttle *Hunter*'s bow rose gracefully before levelling off as the craft began to plane. More than twice the weight of *Water Horse*, she was not as fast, but handled with the same controlled rushing motion. It was exhilarating, swirling through the heat mist caused by the burning sun above. I banked over, then caught a glimpse of White Beach low in the distance, with multi-coloured tents and a row of LMS inflatables pulled up on the shingle. Quite obviously the whole operation would depend on boats.

Skimming towards them, I could not resist heeling over at the last moment to send a wake arm rolling on the shore, then pulled *Hunter* up in a boil of foam, to drop the hook. It was unnecessary, but I was unrepentant. It was like riding a charger, a great white steed, which bounded forward over the water in response to one's command.

During the next two weeks at Loch Morar the survey team was to enjoy Mediterranean weather, to swelter and sizzle in a heatwave; and actually to bathe in the loch, its gin-clear icewater warmed enough to make it bearable. It was a lovely experience – and perhaps the happiest of all the expeditions; marred only for those ashore by the midges. In the boat I could escape them, but ashore campfire smoke, midge-cream and swishing fronds of bracken could not stop the onslaught. Morar and midges went together, but in spite of them morale remained high, and the suntans developed to a uniform chocolate hue.

In the evenings the whole team would eat together ashore by the tented encampment, strewn about with equipment, then indulge in a game of 'Frisbee'. One of the crew was a young medical doctor from Edinburgh, who was expert with this strange aerodynamic toy and sent it skimming in all directions.

Morar in 1972 was one of those blissful interludes, and as we made long excursions in *Hunter* to Swordlands, and Meoble, and Lettermora Bay, and to the head of the loch with its great mountain clefts, no two days were quite the same. Technically, it was not a success, with equipment failures and errors of judgment to contend with – but as if to make up for this, Elizabeth Montgomery Campbell, who had done so much for the LMS, had a good back sighting in clear daylight. As principal author of the book *The Search for Morag*, Liz had chronicled the sighting record, which she had researched with meticulous care and truthfulness – but from the standpoint of an academic. Now she was faced with the reality of a sighting, which caused her to think deeply about it. As a result she wrote to the Scottish Nature Conservancy Board, stating the facts of her experience. She could do no more than that, as there had been no other witness.

The problem of supply at Morar was more acute than at Loch Ness, and each day a party would motor into Mallaig, the fishing port. The year before on one of these visits I heard of a most unusual catch brought in by a trawler – a giant sea turtle, weighing 'thirteen hundredweight'. Disbelieving, I tracked it down. Squeezing between two old wooden storage sheds, and peering through the cobwebs of a window, I could see an immense reptilian head, and as my pupils enlarged to suit the gloom the whole carapace was outlined. Resting on a bed of scattered chips of ice was the body of a giant leathery turtle. I was dumbfounded – the animal had at least three times the bulk of the specimen on display in the British Natural History

M

Museum. Two bloody gashes across its back showed where a pro-peller blade had struck and killed it. It was a colossus, weighing perhaps 1,500 pounds, the biggest sea turtle I had ever seen in my life. I rushed back to Loch Morar to gain the support of a marine zoologist. It was obvious that the creature should be preserved, but there was no one about – the crews were away down the loch. Next day the turtle had gone, shipped south no doubt for turtle soup and a handsome profit. There was no means of finding out who owned it, or where it had been sent. It was just another load of fishy produce to dispose of quickly. No one had considered its scientific value.

In the hubbub of commercial activity at the port men had jobs to do and if there was money to be made, they made it. No one could blame them. The reality of this situation was brought home to me again at Mallaig in 1972. A small, stocky, professional diver was working on the bed of the harbour, an air hose spewing bubbles in a great upsurge of water. Ashore an old compressor roared to charge the tanks which supplied him through an airline. Two tousled grimy youths lounged about reading comics; these were his helpers, ignoring the shuddering equipment – the gauges with broken glass. Again, professionalism – rough and tough, but working. No room for niceties.

Returning home via Achnahannet, I parked the boat before driving south by car. I just had time to say hello to Bob Rines who had flown over for new experiments, little realizing that within a week an absolutely crucial underwater result would be achieved by him.

I had business to attend to, before returning for another stint in *Hunter* and two weeks of solitary drifting on Loch Ness.

At home, Bob Rines rang me to say that in the early hours of 8 August, on Urquhart Bay, his sonar-chart machine had recorded very large echoes of something moving through the water at close range, and that the flashing strobe-light camera had been down in the target area. I met him at London airport and examined the traces. He promised to keep me informed about the film when it was developed in America.

My family had planned to go to the south coast for their holiday as they had spent five weeks at Achnahannet the year before and wanted a change. We departed south and north respectively on the same day, but after eleven hours at the wheel I found myself back home again with oil pressure trouble on the Mark 8 Jaguar. It was infuriating but there was no point in wrecking the veteran car, because *Hunter* would be immobilized without it.

Awaiting the repairs, I heard from another Japanese TV group who wanted to make a film at Loch Ness, and after the usual garbled phone calls from Tokyo I agreed to help on a 'first come over' basis. Experience had shown that problems sorted themselves out once the team had arrived. I returned to Loch Ness for a spell in *Hunter*, then flew back to meet them at London airport; a director, a camera man and a student interpreter.

It was clear that the film they wanted to shoot was about the mystery, as seen through the eyes of a child. Angus, my youngest son, then eleven years old was chosen to play the part, much to his delight.

For a week we indulged the art and science of making films, aboard *Hunter* and ashore in the mountains, and at Urquhart Castle. Angus 'interviewed' Alex Campbell, the retired water bailiff. It was an attractive scene – the wise old gentleman quietly replying to the small boy's questions, while in the background the artistic Japanese adjusted lights and cameras, interpreting instructions from staccato Japanese.

The *Navpros* team shot the *Hunter* operation in detail from inside and outside the boat, at night, filming through the windows. The camera men wore carpet slippers, even when climbing up the mountains. The director made the plans, and the interpreter did his best to put them into English. Sign language filled in the details. It was an interesting experience, and as the weather continued to be kind, the patchwork of light and shade effects at Loch Ness and the mists at dawn were duly recorded.

Home once more, after a trip by sleeper on the Royal Highlander from Inverness, we relaxed, agreeing that film making was good fun, but hard work. Angus returned to school with his reputation much enhanced; and I had to explain his absence in a letter to the teacher. I wrote a note stating that 'Angus has been playing the star role in a Japanese film about the Loch Ness Monster', which sounded improbable. I explained too that rare opportunities like this should not be missed, from an educational viewpoint. It seemed to do the trick.

Back once more by air, I boarded *Hunter* at the Abbey Haven, intent on making a final journey round the loch – a grand tour of all its nooks and crannies, drifting and sailing as much as possible, and taking a week in the process. It was the first time I had covered the 50 miles of water in this way, and with the marvellous autumn colours it promised to be rewarding.

Twice during the summer's work I had been close to large water disturbances, and there was always the chance the animal would surface. With the equipment I had aboard, if this happened, the great monster-hunt would be brought to its conclusion.

I set sail at two knots behind the spinnaker I had rigged from poles attached to the pulpit railing – a third of the old camouflaged bell tent, which cost me precisely nothing. It worked well, and was self-steering downwind. I set course on the outboard skeg, which acted like a rudder.

Hunter spent the winter ashore at Fort Augustus on a trailer, tucked into the garden of a friend's house. She was safe there from the attentions of 'visitors', a gang of whom had stolen boats and motors the summer before, moored in Inchnacardoch Bay. Thefts of this kind were almost unheard of at Loch Ness, but with the ever-increasing flood of visitors the days of trust had gone for ever.

I had checked on the boat in the early spring of 1973, on another brief film-making visit; and as life in her had been so pleasant the year before I planned to go on the water for two months, beginning in May. I had visions of catching the dry weather and sun, and the quiet which preceded holidays. Cruisers were beginning to appear on Loch Ness, touring through the canal system and although they were relatively quiet in passage, when they dropped anchor for the night there was noise from the occupants, who were on holiday, and who wanted to fish or splash about in dinghies. Monster-watching with any sort of artificial disturbance was a complete waste of time.

On the way north, I stopped off to lecture to the joint Biological Societies of Edinburgh and Heriot Watt Universities, then motored on to spend the night with friends at Urquhart Bay, before launching.

I arrived just as Loch Ness had been 'exorcized' by an English clergyman, the Reverend Dr Donald Omand, who had conducted the ceremony at the extremities of the loch and at other appropriate places. He was of the opinion that dark influences were at work, and that the phenomenon of the Monster had a bad effect on the people who chose to pursue it – it caused 'mental instability'.

Having performed this quite serious ritual, he then re-enacted it for the benefit of the BBC, who televised him, adding comments of their own, and from local people. Understandably, the majority treated the matter lightly. I watched the TV programme then departed west to start my own lonely operations.

I was not inclined to scoff at Dr Omand, or those associated with him, though I could hardly subscribe to the belief that the Monster was a phantom. Having seen and filmed it I knew otherwise, but where the dark forces were concerned, if Dr Omand believed it was possible to rid the place of them he deserved to be given a respectful hearing.

During the long years of my search I had met a great number of people, a few of whom claimed to have psychic gifts. Not all of them were right in what they guessed, or interpreted – but in one or two cases they had been completely right, and I had experienced several 'coincidences', which were outside the mathematical realms of chance.

This did not mean, however, that one could afford to stop being practical in whatever was attempted. When living on the water, one's very life depended on it.

The day I launched *Hunter* in May 1973, this fact was brought home to me by a tragic accident:

Letter home

Aboard *Hunter*
out of Ft. Augustus
Loch Ness.
May 31st 1973.

'On Saturday 19th May, I launched at Inchnacardoch Bay, with the help of two pleasant young men camping in vehicles at the lay-by. One was fishing, with his own boat, and the other had an enormously powerful hydroplane, which he was testing out. It did about 70 m.p.h. and looked pretty dangerous to me. While in the usual slow process of unloading gear, and preparing *Hunter* for the slip, two men arrived on the scene with a tiny wooden canoe. By now the good weather was over, and a high wind was whipping up the whitecaps. The younger man, in his mid-twenties, I should say, told me he had built the canoe himself. I warned him of the dread danger of capsizing into the ice-water of the Ness, and the thirty-five–forty minutes to unconsciousness if unable to get one's body clear of the water; but he paid no attention. I must have had a presentiment, because I kept on about the risks, thinking he would probably tell me to mind my own business. Finally, I asked him if he had flares to let off to attract attention, if he went over. He replied saying he sometimes carried them when canoeing in the *sea* – in short, as the Ness was only a loch he did not think it warranted them. He then paddled off in the canoe, which was scarcely visible.

About an hour later he was found floating in his lifejacket, dead, and was towed into Ft. Augustus by a fisherman. He had capsized.

Just after launching *Hunter*, I went to test the engine and controls, only to find the boat being blown into the very shallow mud end of the bay . . . with both anchors down! One of my helpers and I battled to pole out with oars, but it was almost impossible. What a way to start – we were exhausted, and I could see us being stuck in the mud until the wind abated. Finally, over a pocket of deeper water I went into reverse, and literally ploughed a way out through the silt, which fortunately is very soft. We then motored round to the Abbey Jetty, where sailboats, a big new safety launch and other canoes were all out on the, by now, very rough water. Of course we did not know of the tragedy – and I enjoyed watching the boys from the Abbey School all having an exciting time. The sailing dinghy capsized, the safety launch fouled a mooring with its prop, and stalled; my own inflatable, borrowed to help with the salvage, got blown away, and about half the boys somehow ended up in the loch themselves.

The net result was a collection of shivering young men, all rushing about helping, and shouting instructions, or falling in. Hence the term 'messing about with boats' which is what we all do most of the time when out in them. It is inescapable.

The next day was typical Ness, with a strong easterly, and bitterly cold. I headed up-loch, determined to get rid of landsman's qualms that beset one when first back on the water. Going strong through the waves with plenty of power, I stepped down into the cabin to arrest some clattering object, only to be flung off my feet and crack my head on the door-frame. It almost knocked me out, and I got back into the cockpit for once thanking my 'stars' . . . which saved the boat and myself from the threat of a second disaster. *Hunter*, under power, in waves like that, without a helmsman would have either rolled over, or ploughed into the rocks. I came back wondering when things would begin to go right. They always do seem to go wrong at the start of expeditions. . . . '

Contrary to expectations, and the experience of the year before, during the next two months the weather continued foul, with torrents of rain and rough water. The old Mark 8 Jaguar which I had bought originally for £40 failed the Ministry of Transport Test, and was held up for six weeks awaiting parts. This confined me to the boat, and the tiny wet living space it presented. Condensation ruined my films, and all five of my cameras were blown off the cabin roof to clatter on the deck.

Ashore, a series of grim human disasters occurred. There were murders, suicides, and fatal car accidents along the north shore road. In the loch two more people were drowned. It was as though some awesome shadow had cast itself upon the Ness. There was even a report of a weird psychic manifestation following the exorcism –

or some extraordinary natural effect, for which there was no explanation. These events had a sobering influence, and the opinion grew amongst monster-hunters that things had been 'stirred up'.

For my own part, I continued operations, applying the rules of common sense. The moment I relaxed these I put my life in danger. Twice I nearly 'bought it'. Once crossing the loch in big waves, I picked up a roller transversely and began to surf. *Hunter* tipped over to the point where equipment fell off the shelves. She was on her beam ends at 20 knots, before she righted.

Again, in rough and squally weather, I was moving down from Foyers, under power – too much power to get the journey done and my numbed extremities back into the cabin – when the small voice of common sense told me to throttle down – I did, and within twenty seconds hit the reef off Johnnie's Point. There were three shattering crashes as the outboard skeg kicked up. Had I struck under greater power, the back end would have come off the boat and the heavy fibreglass hull, with everything inside it, would have sunk in a trice. Glass boats have no inherent buoyancy.

As if to remind one of the need for caution at this place, just around the point the wreck of old *Narwhal* lay bleaching in the sun.

In 1971 we had bought her from the Abbey Sailing Club for use with the LNI. She was in a poor way, but the timbers were sound beneath the rust and peeling paintwork. Scraping and re-furbishing was done ashore, then with the help of the boys, the LNI crew, boats, ropes and the advice of onlookers the herculean task of launching her was accomplished over rollers. Once in the loch she was towed to Inchnacardoch and a deck house built up, then up-loch to Urquhart Bay, where she completed fitting out.

Narwhal had a long history, starting life as a ship's lifeboat on the old Cunarder *Britannic*. She was sold, and converted as a two-master to sail off the Western Isles; and from there back into the Ness.

Her recovery and subsequent use by the LNI in 1971 and 1972 had produced many excitements, and long exploratory journeys up and down the loch. She was big enough for a crew to sleep aboard, and solid enough to withstand a Loch Ness gale, but in the winter of 1972 when anchored off Johnnie's Point she dragged the hook in a storm, and was pounded to bits on the rocks. It was a sad loss.

In early July, after flying home for a few days respite, and to see the family, I returned to Loch Ness to meet Bob Rines and the new Academy team, who had just flown in from Kenya, where they had been filming an eclipse. They brought with them new devices to install as an underwater sonar-camera station.

By good fortune Ivor Newby arrived with *Kelpie*, which he launched and drove at speed to Urquhart Bay. I followed in *Hunter* under bowsail – or 'snoutsail' as I preferred to call it, stopping overnight at Foyers. In her camouflage *Hunter* was truly difficult to see.

Ivor and I had spent so much time on the water in boats that it was good to have his company and his help in getting the station down. It was a complicated operation. Wing-commander Cary's yacht *Smuggler* acted as station boat above the rig, which was an odd contrivance with scaffolding, lights, sonars and cameras, and yards of heavy cabling. Assembled ashore it was floated out, then lowered into position with the help of divers.

Everything went splendidly, and then a north-easter blew up 5 ft waves which pushed *Smuggler* off station, pulled the cables taut, and up-ended the station underwater. There was no time to wait for calmer weather, so we put down a second mooring block and cable in deep water, and by the time the American scientists had left, everything was back in place again; whereupon the electronics went haywire, and during the next six weeks resisted all adjustments. It was another irritation – and as I had not even seen a disturbance that summer, on 30 July I reluctantly dragged *Hunter* out and towed her south, sleeping two nights on the road in her.

In all, since 1968 in three different craft – *Cizara*, *Water Horse* and *Hunter* – I had spent 240 days and nights alone on the vast, mysterious, lonely pools of Loch Ness and Loch Morar, which I had come to love and know, as perhaps no Englishman had known in all their history.

17
The
technological net

In the Mediterranean, at a certain time of the year local fishermen venture out and lay a net. This is then pulled in from shore, slowly and laboriously, inch by inch with everybody helping. People of the villages come down to pull on the net, adding their puny individual strength to the whole, which inexorably brings in the catch – the tunny – giant fish which thrash about explosively as the net encloses them.

At Loch Ness today, and to a lesser extent at Loch Morar, the nets are out, comprising an exquisitely fine mesh of technology. Their purpose is to bring in whatever is in these lochs for inspection and identification. In this there is a difference from the tunny fishers, whose object is to kill.

The 'catch' in both these places will ensure the safety of the netted creatures as no other fishing operation will. The whole object of the voluntary effort is to establish the reality of the phenomenon of the monsters, as they are known to everyone, and thus to introduce a nationally-sponsored research and study programme.

One can argue tediously about the pros and cons of scraps of evidence – of photographs, films, sonar-recordings and their meanings – but if an objective view is taken and the facts concerning them are studied, and admitted, there is enough evidence already to establish reality.

What we do not have enough of at the present time is detail, from which to eliminate the various alternative theories as to what these monsters can be. Until we obtain this detail, or catch a specimen (which is not impossible) we can only theorize about them.

The most exciting aspect of the search and research programmes is that the work is open to individuals who become interested in it, and who wish to contribute their knowledge, and talents. There is no bar to them, and whereas there is a frontier to science and always will be, this search is not a closed frontier to people.

With the passage of time it has become obvious that the problem at Loch Ness is a very difficult one. There is no easy or quick solution – and it would be foolish to pretend otherwise. The work and effort that has gone into finding a solution is already prodigious, and whereas the monsters do not yet officially exist, more and more qualified people in authority are privately coming to realize that they in fact do; and that it is time to put an end to all the nonsense; to accept finally a very great discovery, the honour for which goes to no single individual, or even group of people, but to all the unselfish hundreds who have pulled upon the net. The researchers, the expeditioners, the scientists, the students, the helpers, the Highlanders, the press and TV people and the countless ordinary folk who have had the courage to stand up and speak the truth about a sighting.

Looking ahead, we can only guess at what will happen, but if the trend continues and the power of our modern technology is brought to bear, the problem can be resolved in one of several ways – by clearly definitive photography at close range on the surface, or underwater; by obtaining a small tissue sample, or even catching one of the smaller animals; or simply by accumulating all the valid bits of evidence which together tip the scales of science.

It is an absorbing prospect, and if more years go by before the nation realizes what a marvellous part of its natural heritage is contained in Ness and Morar, and perhaps some of the other lochs as well, there is no need to fuss about it. Time is unimportant, and the passage of it can no way affect the outcome, for where truth is involved, the facts stand up; as indeed the people do who recognize them.

Appendix A

In the April 1973 edition of the *Photographic Journal*, the official journal of the Royal Photographic Society of Great Britain, I published an article entitled 'Loch Ness 1972 – the "Rines/Edgerton picture",' the text of which was introduced by a short note from John Sanders, who was then editor. It summarized the results obtained at Loch Ness, and outlined the circumstances which make the sonar-chart recording and underwater photograph shown in plates 22 and 23 so important.

In the March 1970 issue of The Photographic Journal, *Tim Dinsdale presented a case for serious Monsterhunting, under the title 'The Potential of Photography at Loch Ness'. Since then he has run two summer-long photo expeditions for the Loch Ness Investigation Bureau as Surface-photography Director; and in 1972 spent three months on private operations aboard* Hunter, *a specially-adapted photographic boat. Altogether he has been involved at Loch Ness with fieldwork since 1960 and is thus in a position to bring information up to date....* ED.

In years past, the cry at Loch Ness would be – 'Where is your scientific evidence?' Today, no one who is aware of the facts concerning the phenomenon of the 'Monster', and the results obtained from recent probings, would bother to ask the question. He would know that, since 1966, reports have been published which are scientifically based, analysing the results of photographic work above and below the surface and the sonar contacts obtained – indicating large midwater moving objects – the echoes from which are not apparently spurious or from any known species of fish.

To establish credibility, and to gain a sense of perspective, it is useful to list these more important results starting with the RAF's Joint Air Reconnaissance Intelligence Centre Report on the film I shot of the Monster at Loch Ness, in 1960. This report, which was published as an HMSO document in 1966, accepts the film as genuine and as showing an object which moved at some 10 m.p.h. – a cross-section through which would be at least 6 feet wide and 5 feet deep. As it submerged during the course of the film and travelled half a mile without a propeller wash, it was clearly animate.

In 1967, Richard Raynor obtained a short sequence of 35mm black and white film through one of the Loch Ness Investigation Bureau's ultra long-range ciné cameras. It showed a big V-wash moving on calm water, which ceased when *Scot II*, a local passenger boat, appeared in frame, proving the locality beyond a doubt. The RAF analysis found a 7-foot object at the apex of the wash, just breaking surface.

In 1968, Professor D. Gordon Tucker and Hugh Braithwaite of the University of Birmingham tried out a new type of digital sonar at Loch Ness over a period of two weeks. Filmed recordings of the display showed echoes from large moving objects, the behaviour of which ruled out fish.

In 1969, Robert E. Love, Jr, sponsored by Field Enterprise of Chicago in conjunction with the Loch Ness Investigation (LNI) obtained more contacts, using a Honeywell sonar mounted at the bows of a patrolling boat. Both these sets of photographed results were published by the LNI in its 1968 and 1969 Annual Reports.

In 1970, a small team of sonar experts from the Academy of Applied Science, Belmont, Mass., including its president, Dr Robert H. Rines, and the designer of a highly definitive sidescan sonar, Dr Martin Klein, obtained more clear contacts in both the static and mobile sonar modes. These were described at a national news conference in London, and after further analysis details were published by Klein in the USA.

In 1971 calibration tests were run in Loch Ness and Loch Morar by the Academy/LNI teams using a flashing strobe-light

ciné camera underwater, working on the time-lapse principle.
In the spring, at the Academy's invitation, I had talked about
the research to audiences in America and Professor Harold
Edgerton, Hon. FRPS, pioneer of strobe-light photography had
attended. Afterwards he invited us round to his lab at MIT and
promised to put some special gear together. Thus, Bob Rines
was able to obtain photographs even through the peat-stained
soup of Loch Ness in 1971.

In August of 1972, working from boats in Urquhart Bay,
the Edgerton camera was suspended at a depth of some 50 feet.
Nearby, from the LNI's workboat *Narwhal*, a compact
Raytheon sonar-chart recorder scanned the depths surrounding
it.

During the very early hours of 8 August 1972, a large
intruding echo appeared on the Raytheon chart, and remained
in the vicinity of the sonar transducer and the strobe-camera
which was flashing every 15 seconds. It was moving, and fish
echoes which came up as tiny dots on the chart turned into
streaks as the fish swam away from it.

The 16mm film cassette was subsequently removed, flown
back to the USA and developed under bond by Eastman-Kodak.
In several frames, coincident with the sonar trace, a large but
indistinct body had imposed itself.

Next, the sonar chart was submitted for analysis to no less
than five separate authorities – and the film duly 'computer
enhanced' by the same process used to clarify some spectacular
pictures from space, most recently in the case of the Mariner
unmanned probes to the planet Mars.

In one frame of the film there is a remarkable improvement,
showing what appears to be a huge paddle-like structure – an
obvious limb; the conservative photo optical measurements of
which establish a length of 6–8 feet and a width of 2–4 feet.
It was photographed at near to maximum range, which in the
impenetrable gloom of Loch Ness water is about 20 feet.

In view of the inescapable reality of this underwater picture
(and its stunning significance) comment is superfluous; unless it
is to pay credit to the technical brilliance and sheer persistence

of the two Americans who helped to make it possible. In this connection, and in keeping with a now established Loch Ness tradition, the picture deserves an identifying title.

I can think of no better one than the 'Rines/Edgerton picture'.

Appendix B

Activities of the Academy of Applied Science
by Robert H. Rines, President

The humanistic involvement in the search for the large animals in Loch Ness is perhaps as intriguing as the scientific and adventure aspects.

Hardly a week passes without the Boston-based (Massachusetts) office of the Academy of Applied Science receiving an inquiry from a science class of a primary or secondary school or college, or a request for material from an individual student or other member of the public-at-large; or a status question from the press and other media. Often this is supplemented by voluntary suggestions of techniques, or proposals such as that of a five-year-old lad who had heard of the biologically clean nature of the Ness and wondered whether the loan of Nessie was feasible to 'klene up the polatints in the grate lakes'.

The linking of our American team, operating under the auspices of the Academy, with Tim Dinsdale's program, and the former activities of the British Loch Ness Investigation Bureau, is a story of warm friendship and common interests in a project designed to solve a great human-interest problem that could expand human knowledge.

For the Academy, however, with its interdisciplinary concern with the interfaces of science and law, this is a continued experiment in testing science's general unwillingness to learn how to appraise and evaluate eyewitness evidence, as compared with the law's considerable trust and reliance on the same.

The ever-improving (though painfully slow) results that we are

N

collectively obtaining in the investigation at Loch Ness, may well serve as a starting point for a new attitude on the part of the scientific community towards the importance of (1) learning how to use oral testimony in the search for scientific truth and of (2) maintaining open-mindedness (though it may be too much to expect a collective ability to dream creatively).

It is in that spirit, that a 'Who's Who' of eminent American scientists, engineers, businesses, universities and even governmental agencies have, sometimes openly and more often unofficially, given encouragement, equipment and advice to the Academy team, bringing sophisticated technological aids to bear in the common search, and efforts to identify the large aquatic animals in the loch.

Renowned sonar and electronic experts have planned vacations and business trips in order to join the experiments for a few days, and/or have loaned apparatus, much of it specially designed, to fathom the physical nature of this giant body of water and its bays, and its angular bottom and cavernous or undercut rocky marginal ledges – possible lairs of the animals. One-of-a-kind, special underwater, intense light strobe and elapsed-time moving picture camera apparatus has been provided, also novel miniature computer-controlled moving-object-discriminating sonar and underwater lighting and camera systems, designed only to operate if very large moving objects of predetermined minimum size are within camera range, in the murky, dark waters. Each year, this equipment is improved in the light of the frailties and inadequacies shown by the previous year's tests; and we feel we are zeroing in on the ultimate answer. Among the continuing contributors have been MIT's Dr Harold E. Edgerton and Jan Olaf Willums, Martin Klein of Klein Associates, Charles Adams of Raytheon, Isaac S. Blonder of Blonder Tongue Laboratories, Duane Marshall of United States Scientific Instruments, Charles Wyckoff of Applied Photo Sciences, Vickers Oceanics with their PC submersibles, numerous Academy associates including the late Dr Laurence S. Foster, Robert and Dr Joan Needleman, and Carol, Ann and Rob Rines, Lee Frank, and innumerable English and Scottish friends, among them Murray Stewart, Nick Witchell, former RAF Wing Commander Basil Cary and Winifred Cary, Donald Cameron, Ron Bremner and Commander Bodie, who have united with their boats and their skippering expertise – and Alec Menzies who has been generous in providing his pier and facilities for a base of operations.

Ancillary experiments including possible attractants, ranging from pheromones and foods to US Navy-recorded sounds of the underwater life of the world, have also been conducted with the support and contributions of an army of experts in these areas, including representatives of the Universities of Rhode Island and Miami, the Miami Seaquarium, the Harvard Medical School, the US Army Natick Laboratories, Tufts University, International Flavors and Fragrances of New Jersey, Food and Chemical Research of Seattle, Washington, and others.

The deleterious effects of hoaxes and undesirable publicity on public institutions, including the British Museum and the Smithsonian Institute, seem now to have been dissipated, and co-operative analytical assistance has been offered and received. Similarly, critical independent analyses of our underwater sonar and photographic successes to date have been forthcoming from experts in the leading corporate, university and government sectors in these fields; and we have been relying upon such a jury to pass on all the evidence we collect.

Hopefully, the time is very near when the proper investigators from the Admiralty and oceanographic institutions, with the required highly expensive underwater systems, will feel sufficiently free of adverse public reaction, to assist in attaining the final and irrefutable identification of these animals.

Appendix C

At the time of writing in March 1974 it is of interest to note that a second underwater photo from the series of five obtained in Urquhart Bay in 1972 has responded to computer analysis, and that this will be made the subject of another *Photographic Journal* article. In a letter to me dated 26 February 1974, Dr Rines commented:

> Now, for the very good news that the people at JPL [Jet Propulsion Laboratories] in California were most excited with the improvement of what we thought to be a 'tail' photo in our previous series. I have not yet seen the several different computer analyses of our improved pictures, though I understand that they were able to remove all of the silt cloud particles without impairing target information. The preliminary telephone message is that they see both a good view of an edge on flipper and an apparent second animal body behind with what looks like appendages.

With the fast approaching new monster-hunting season it is evident that future operations will be resumed with enthusiasm, both by the American contingent, and the indigenous searchers, who are beginning to polish up their lenses. For my own part I look forward to a resumption of work in *Water Horse*, this small craft having been salvaged from the cloying mud and degradation of canal waters. In 1974 it is *Hunter* which will be held in reserve – while I drift, and sail, and nose a quiet way into the more inaccessible deep water places of Lochs Ness and Morar, and watch over these lochs from the stable platform of a tripod mounted high up on the shoreline – for it is variety of action, and technique, which proves the most rewarding. If a photographic confrontation develops, it could be from the cockpit of *Water Horse*, I suspect, and fittingly, for she is already full of history, and will remain at Loch Ness henceforward.

But, if the Monster does not surface within camera range of a boat patrol – the possibility of a long-range shore-based camera station 'nailing' it is real. The odds against this happening are very, very long, as all the years of watching have shown, but the criticism that this technique has failed does not do justice to it. More correctly, it has 'failed to connect decisively', in recent years, but this is simply a measure of the odds.

Any good surfacing can be recorded by a telephoto shore-based camera, provided the watcher is alert, and is able to manage his equipment. The LNI practised this technique through ten years of Monster history and today it still has adherents. One of the most persistent, and capable watchers is Nick Witchell, a law student who started first as a schoolboy monster-hunter. During the months of the summer holidays and the long University recess he has watched the loch, and Urquhart Bay in particular, from a base which has come to be known as Nickie's Hut; which he built and equipped with a battery of cameras. If selfless dedication is a measure of the art he deserves to succeed with it, and he may well find a target one day, for on occasion the Beastie does come up – and on very rare occasions more than one of them will surface.

Edinburgh
18th March 1974

Dear Mr. Dinsdale,

I was pleased to receive your letter this morning, and as requested I am enclosing three sketches of the Monsters.

On the morning in September of 1952, my brother and I visited Mr. Chisholm who occupied a croft on the land that my late father then owned. It was a steep climb up from the road and my brother and I paused at the first level piece of ground about half way up, we turned to view the loch and then saw three tracks in the water proceeding at a good speed: about that of a bus or slow car. My brother had a large brass telescope with him (about 40 magnifications) and we took turns to look at the objects. What surprised me at the time was the perfect 'V' formation that was kept without change or drift. The first sighting was at 11 a.m. and continued until 11.20 a.m. There were however slight breaks as we each took turns to look. The tracks continued parallel to the shore for about 17 minutes and were last seen heading straight for the shore where they were screened from view. Unfortunately we did not see them execute the turn inwards. I have drawn the head of the leading one, it was round shaped with what appeared to be small ears or horns and a suggestion of a mouth.

I hope this information will be of help to you.

Yours sincerely,
Kenneth A. Key.

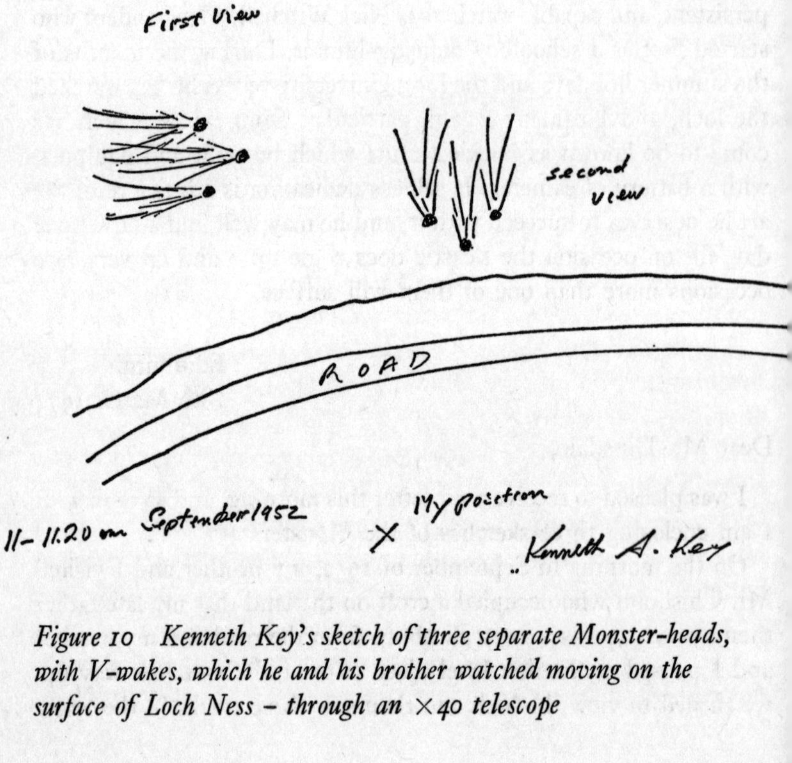

Figure 10   Kenneth Key's sketch of three separate Monster-heads, with V-wakes, which he and his brother watched moving on the surface of Loch Ness – through an ×40 telescope

Over the forty years of Monster history, since it was first 'discovered' in the early 1930s, when the north shore road was built at Loch Ness – there has only been a handful of reports suggesting the presence of more than one animal, and of these multiple reports this is the first 'triple-header' I have heard about. There have been reports of big animals with small ones alongside, and multiple sets of double humps which obviously belong to adult animals of very considerable size.

For example, I recorded on tape an account by the late Mr Connel of the Dores Inn at Loch Ness in 1971, who was a salmon fisher, and in consequence an experienced waterman. He described three pairs of double humps, each pair extending about 20 ft overall, and with water showing between them – which moved slowly in formation, and which submerged together, as though the separate animals were in contact visually underwater. This had occurred in flat-calm misty conditions at a range of half a mile or so. The event took place 'the September before last' which would have made it 1969, and in 1970 a clear sighting, at much closer range, of a large animal on the surface with head and neck upraised was obtained near Fort Augustus, at the other end of the loch. A Mrs Robertson, the local district nurse, and her sister who was a nun from a convent in Germany were both witnesses, in flat-calm sunny conditions, at a range of about 300 yards. The remarkable thing was that a smaller animal followed the big one, with a great to-do and splashing, as though it had difficulty in keeping up. It was a smaller version of the first, but showing only one hump instead of two.

The importance of multiple sightings cannot be overstated, because they indicate the continuing survival of a breeding colony of animals.

In November 1973 I discussed these two latter sightings with Barry Toovey, a producer for BBC Scotland's 'MacLeod at Large' television series. As a result, when we filmed at Loch Ness he interviewed Mrs Robertson, and although the news of Mr Connel's untimely death was a sad disappointment, a co-witness came forward to confirm his story.

Unfortunately, too, Mr Key, whom I had first met in Edinburgh, missed the filming, as I had lost his address. He did not contact me again until March 1974, by which time the TV film had gone out. But when he wrote he followed up with a phone call, and we discussed details of his experience not included in his letter or the sketches. The water had been flat-calm at the time, and the visibility clear. Checking the telescope against an object of known dimensions at about the same range he concluded that the heads were about a foot in size, or presumably slightly larger than a football.

I asked him if he could possibly have been looking at waterbirds, but he dismissed this. The scale was too great. The heads travelled about a mile, and the wake formation was as wide as the length of a bus. In short, waterbirds just did not come into it.

Having talked to Mrs Robertson, Mr Connel, and Mr Key myself, I know they were telling the truth; and as these mature educated people were able to describe their experiences in detail, there is no reason to doubt the accuracy of what they had to say.

The argument that witnesses see what they expect to see, and that distance and light and shade effects delude them, is constantly being put forward by people who have not been to Loch Ness, or talked to witnesses. Undoubtedly mistakes are made, and the most common is that caused by a wake arm from a powerful trawler which has gone by perhaps half an hour before. At water level it can be seen to produce three shadowy 'humps' streaking through the water – and it can fool most people.

However, at really close range, a live animal is a live animal – and if it is very big, there is no mistaking this fact.

In June 1973 when scouting the western reaches of Loch Ness in *Hunter*, I chanced to hear that a group of Abbey school boys had been close to a large animal the year before, near Fort Augustus. After making inquiries I met three of them, and persuaded them to come aboard and record their experience on tape.

The boys, who were boarders at the St Benedict's Catholic public school were Michael McCulloch (14), Michael Caulfield (14), and Ricky Morga (13) – and a fourth, John Eustace, who I did not meet until later. I gained the very definite impression they were not making the story up, because they kept interrupting and correcting each other on minor points of detail. Some of the excitement of the encounter came through on the tape:

Caulfield I began hearing the waves, and then I saw them –
everyone else ignored them –
Self You heard the waves and saw the waves?
C Yes, I stood up. . . . I saw the object going out towards the
middle then it turned towards Borlum Bay – I saw the Monster –
I was that excited –
S But what did you see in fact – what was it like?
C It was of slate colour –
S How long?
C Well we saw about 40 feet but there was still some under
the water –
(*interruption*) I would say about 35 or 30 feet
C But it was very long anyway
(from here on it is difficult to tell which boy was speaking on the
tape due to general excitement, and interrupting voices – but the
comments went as follows):
Self And about how much out of the water?
Boys 2 to 3 feet –
it was only about 10 yards away when we first saw it –
we were at the mouth of the river –
there were ripples coming out from the body, and they started
a wee bit out – they were sort of V-shaped –
S Did you see any head or neck?
Boys No –
S It gave you the impression of great size?
Boys Oh yes (*excitedly*) – the waves were coming – lashing right
on the shore –
S Really?
Boys 2 or 3 foot high waves – it was quite calm elsewhere –
S Now, is there any conceivable chance you were mistaken?
Boys No, no, no boats – nothing at all.
No ships –
S How long did you watch it for?
Boys For about 2 minutes –
S Then what happened?
Boys It just disappeared –
It went down – but one could see the waves turning without any

object on the water.

S Had you believed in it before?

Boys Oh no –

I didn't –

I did, I was the only one who did.

S Do the other boys believe you now?

Boys Well, some of them – (*laughter*).

(We then went inside the cabin of *Hunter*, where I played the tape back, then asked the boys some additional questions.)

S As you were so close you must have seen the texture of the skin – was it skin, or scales, or what?

Boys It was just shiny – sort of wet and shiny.

S You say you saw a disturbance at the side of the body, what was causing this?

Boys We had an argument over that later – but I could have sworn it was some kind of flipper –

Yes.

But I didn't think so –

S The shape on the back – you hear of these humps and bumps and things – did you see any?

Boys There were about three little – there were hardly any humps at all –

There was a long part to the body though . . . one bit seemed to go up – widened up.

S Was that at the front end?

Boys No, the back.

S Did it have any particular sort of movement? Did it go off all as one thing, or did it wriggle or wiggle or what?

Boys At first it did, then it started going up and down to push itself forward – it seemed to go faster when it went up –

Like a caterpillar.

S Like a caterpillar? Humping?

Boys Yes, that's exaggerating, but yes, all the time –

No neck or head appeared, it was just this hump going up and down – just these long hump things.

S And it appeared to be muscular, did it?

Boys Oh yes, it must have been – oh to go that fast!

Yes, and that size –
S What sort of speed?
Boys Well it took two minutes from the mouth of the Oich to the
middle of the loch [about one-third of a mile] and to turn round
towards Borlum Bay –
And about thirty seconds of that, was just watching it – almost
stationary.
S What time of day was this?
Boys One twenty-eight –
No, one twenty-nine –
No, one twenty-eight, it's in my diary, November 13th – clear
flat calm, sunny day. . . .

About a month after this interview, I happened to learn by chance
that the school doctor who lived in Fort Augustus had interviewed
the boys immediately after the event. He was kind enough to cor-
roborate this on my tape, at his house. Dr Edward Buchanan was
convincing too:

Dr Buchanan This occurred on a Monday afternoon – my wife
and I and a friend Mr Hamish Macdonald, games master at the
Abbey School were here – the door bell rang and I went out to
find these four boys, utterly breathless, and really still quite
shaken by the whole incident. Apparently they had run up to the
police station, found nobody there and come straight along;
and said they hoped I didn't mind, but they had to tell
someone. . . . I am convinced these lads were not pulling my leg –
they were just too genuine and they kept it up for too long . . .
we did not actually split them up and take them into different
rooms, but certainly we all talked to different boys and their stories
tallied – they did not have time to make this up and I am utterly
convinced of the genuine nature of this tale.

I was fascinated by it too, because unknown to either Dr Buchanan
or the schoolboys I had previously recorded two other witnesses on
tape who had made remarks which supported points of detail in

their account – but relating to Monsters they had seen on other parts of the loch.

But, before checking back on my library of cassette tapes which I always carried, I moved *Hunter* off to the river mouth, where I often fished, and checked the bottom depth with an accurate *Seascribe* fathometer. This electronic device told me that although on one side the water was shallow, on the other close to where they had seen the creature, it went down to twenty feet immediately offshore – and from there outwards along the shoreline to greater depths. Thus it would have been possible for even a very big animal to approach them within 'ten yards'.

In 1971 I had recorded the late Mr Connel of the Dores Inn, twenty miles up the loch, who had seen three sets of separate double humps one morning on a glassy surface. The humps stood about three feet above the water, and covered about twenty feet, front to rear. Just before these three, separate animals submerged, Mr Connel noticed the humps 'coming together', a sort of muscular heaving motion as they went along.

Could this have been the same reaction the boys had noticed? And could it result from the use of paddles or limbs underwater? It seemed probable, for Newton's Third Law states that for every physical action there is an equal and opposite reaction. In short, if paddles were displacing water rearwards, there would be a surge of power, or thrust reaction forwards. If the humps were situated close to the pelvic and shoulder structures of these animals, they would probably exhibit this marked heaving, surging motion as they moved along.

The boys account suggested this:

S Did it have any particular sort of movement?
Boys At first it did, then it started going up and down to push itself forward – it seemed to go faster when it went up –
Like a caterpillar.

This remark, 'it seemed to go faster when it went up', fits the mechanical picture – the physical reaction to a rearward paddle-stroke with a thrustline vector throwing the hump forward and up. The bow of a racing-eight on the River Thames can be seen to 'go faster' momentarily, to surge forward as the crew puts in a power-stroke with their oars, but as the boat is not a flexible structure it does not hump upwards too, 'like a caterpillar'.

This comment, had brought a tingle of excitement – an electric shock of interest to me when the boys had made it, because unknown to them I had recorded an elderly Highland lady's account the year before, in which she had described seeing one of these creatures out of water many years ago, in which she used the same expression.

'Out of water' reports were extremely rare, but they nevertheless existed. In all the years of my search I had only met two people who claimed this mind-boggling experience. The first was now dead, but I had known him personally, and his account and sketches had appeared in my first book *Loch Ness Monster* in 1961, and again in *The Story of the Loch Ness Monster*, which was published for young people in 1973. Torquil MacLeod had been a man of wide experience, and possessed a finely educated mind. I liked, and trusted him, and believed his report of the great long-necked animal he had watched lying on the shore partly out of water, on 28 February 1960. He had viewed it across the loch near the Horse Shoe scree, for a period of nine minutes; and had been able to measure it roughly through graticulated binocular lenses. His estimated 'visible length' was between 45 and 50 ft. The creature had huge rear paddles, and 'large squarish ended flippers' forward of them, which he saw distinctly, when the Monster turned to heave itself back into the water.

Of the 'out of water' reports, of which a dozen or so were more than hearsay, Torquil's was the most dramatic, if not the most recent. That distinction went to the LNI in 1963, when a dark neck-like object was filmed in colour at a range of over two miles. When analysed by the RAF long-range photographic experts, the object (which was too far away for the telephoto lens to show up detail) – was estimated to be 17 ft long. Presumably the remainder of the body was still in the water.

The Highland lady witness, to whom I was introduced in 1972 had lived in Fort Augustus all her life, and when a child of eleven, had seen the Monster out of water in broad daylight, heaving its great bulk out of the wooded perimeter of Inchnacardoch Bay, where it re-entered the water. She was seventy-four when I recorded her account, but could remember the incident, and the fright it had given her as though it was yesterday.

Reports of this Inchnacardoch 'children's' sighting of so many years ago have become confused in the record with a date of 1919 attributed to it by Constance Whyte in *More Than a Legend*; and 1912 and 1919, as two separate incidents with different casts – 'William Macgruer and others' and 'Mrs Cameron and brothers' – by Peter Costello in his book *In Search of Lake Monsters*.

If Mrs Cameron's memory serves her correctly, it must have been 1909, and the confusion of names has resulted from the fact that she assumed the name of Cameron when she married.

Excerpts from her marvellous verbatim account make interesting reading:

And this is my sister who was in the pram at the time [laughter]; well then my dear, it was a Sunday afternoon about twenty past four, and we were going for a walk down as far as the Cherry Island, a little past the Inchnacardoch Hotel.

Mrs Cameron, then eleven years old was pushing the pram with her baby sister and they sat down on the shore of Inchnacardoch Bay, a small inlet of water from the main loch, with a flat silted bottom shelving away into deep water from the periphery of swampy grass, bushes and trees. She said there were 'four or five of us' children, and before long they began to skip stones across the water.

The bay on those days had no road close to it, no boats with outboard motors, and was smaller and more heavily wooded than today – where it is used as an anchorage for yachts, and rumbles to the passage of trucks, and motors. The water level was lower too, due, she thought, to the recent dams built by the Hydroelectric Development Board.

When, my dear, what an awful rustling noise was coming out of the trees – when you walk in a wood you know how you can sort of hear things crackling, and the breaking of old branches – well this was the same as that – as if it was splitting and breaking of the branches of the trees themselves – so of course we looked, and the loch was quite calm, and there couldn't be any wind knocking the trees, you see, when – oh, my dear, out of the trees came this *huge* thing! Broad, broad, here. . . . I saw it deliberately lift one leg and put it into the water – and thinking of the baby – well I was eleven years of age, and thinking of herself, I just grabbed her, I didn't wait to see the end of it, or the rest of it coming out of the trees which was – have you ever seen a caterpillar walking on a cabbage leaf? That's what it seemed to be, like that – I saw two of its big parts, and that was quite enough, because it was a huge thing – I hadn't seen an elephant in them days, but I've seen one since – and that was the colour. The colour of an elephant.

The children ran off home, pushing the pram as fast as they could go – and when they told their parents about it, their grandfather warned them not to discuss the matter, as he believed they had seen the Devil – because they had been out picking nuts on the Sabbath day. Quite evidently, he was not joking.

The memory of this experience was obviously still very clear to Mrs Cameron, and together with Murray Stewart, another monster-hunter of long experience, I questioned her in detail about it. She had seen no long neck, but as she explained, the creature was coming directly towards them and they couldn't tell if it had one or not. The forelimb was thicker than an elephant's and 'stumped' at the end. She held up a big frying pan, to indicate the end of it, and said it was bigger than that. This called to mind Torquil's comment that he had seen 'a large squarish ended flipper forward of the big rear paddles'. But he was looking through binoculars across the loch – a distance of nearly a mile.

It was a pity the children had not seen the whole creature entering the bay – before they took to flight, but as we drove Mrs Cameron round for her to show us the exact spot – it could not have been more than 120 yards from where they were standing. As it appeared to be heading directly for them, their terror could be understood.

I questioned Mrs Cameron as to whether she could have mistaken a big bull, coming to the water for a drink for the Monster – in reply she said: 'Oh, my dear, no, we were brought up with cows and horses, and I've never seen anything like it – or since.' She said, too, that it was about as wide as 'an elephant and a half' and about 'as high as myself' from the ground.

Quite recently Mrs Cameron had collected Brooke Bond picture cards, from tea packets, showing prehistoric animals, and had selected one which seemed to be the closest. This had been passed to another Scottish lady at Strone, whom I knew well, and I had viewed it a few weeks before. It showed a brontosaurus.

Whatever the precise facts of the case might be, it was obvious to us that Mrs Cameron could remember her experience clearly – and a few days later I moored *Hunter* in the bay one glorious sunny afternoon, and went exploring the marshy perimeter in the dinghy. I stepped ashore, to wander through the maze of scrub and bushes – and as I did, I noticed how the dry twigs and branches snapped and cracked as I forced a passage through them. It was a most noticeable sound.

Appendix D

Subject literature

For adult readers
The Loch Ness Monster and Others, Rupert T. Gould, Geoffrey Bles (1934).
More Than a Legend, Constance Whyte, MB, BS, Hamish Hamilton (1957).
Loch Ness Monster, Tim Dinsdale, ARAeS, Routledge & Kegan Paul (1961) and Chilton Books, Philadelphia (1962); updated new edition in paperback and hard covers, Routledge & Kegan Paul (1972).*
The Elusive Monster, Maurice Burton, DSc, Rupert Hart-Davis (1961).
The Leviathans, Tim Dinsdale, Routledge & Kegan Paul (1966), and (as *Monster Hunt*) an enlarged new edition by Acropolis Books, Washington, DC (1972).*
The Great Orme of Loch Ness, F. W. Holiday, Faber (1968).*
The Search for Morag, Elizabeth Montgomery Campbell and David Solomon, PHD, Tom Stacey (1972), and Walker, New York (1973).*
The Dragon and the Disc, F. W. Holiday, Sidgwick & Jackson (1973) and W. W. Norton, New York (1973).*
In Search of Lake Monsters, Peter Costello, Garnstone Press (1974).*
The Loch Ness Story, Nicholas Witchell, Terence Dalton (1974).*

For young people
The Story of the Loch Ness Monster, Tim Dinsdale, Target Books (paperback) (1973),* and Allan Wingate (hard covers) (1973).*

* Indicates book is currently in print.

Supplement

At the time of correcting the proofs of this book, in December 1974, the opportunity has arisen to include some interesting new information on the summer's monster-hunting activities, and some results, which were completely unexpected.

Predictably, in June and July 1974 I returned to the search in little *Water Horse*, spending another forty-six days and nights in her. My absurd affection for this battered, but elegant hull in fibreglass had at last been consummated. I owned it now, and with a 20 h.p. Mercury on loan from Jim Ewing she was economical to operate, and could cruise at low speed all day without refuelling – which was to prove useful for sonar work later in the summer.

In July I travelled south for a few days, then flew back to resume action when Wolper Productions from the USA made a TV documentary for world-wide release – and for a day or two I chased around the loch fixing interviews and acted parts in demonstration. I put out for them in *Water Horse* from Fort Augustus, before returning to the Academy's experimental base at Urquhart Bay.

The weather was fine, too hot almost, though not for a Californian Academy member, who had done the computer work on the 'flipper' and other photographs. Alan Gillespie was a tall, bronzed west-coast American. We had first met at JPL in Pasadena in 1972, when Bob Rines made the introductions. We talked about his work, and the remaining underwater photographs which he was still examining. They were real, but the outlines of shapes in the peaty water remained as difficult to interpret accurately.

By now the Academy's underwater station, damaged a few days earlier, had been repaired, but the computer was giving trouble and Dr Rines decided to postpone this particular experiment. Instead, he came out with me in *Water Horse*, bringing with him a new Raytheon deep-ocean sonar chart recorder which he wanted to try out.

We traversed the bay, and then the loch, to find clear detail coming up on the chart. Chasms, mounts and fissures, and then the great flat plain of silt across the bottom of Loch Ness, which appeared in all the charts.

But we saw something else too, which was incredible – echoes from the sound pulse coming up from *beneath* the bottom silt, from more than 1,000 ft beneath it, outlining the subterranean shape of the rock-walls of the Great Glen Fault. If these indications were not from some sort of double echo it could mean we were the first human beings to see this dramatically exciting geological feature – a discovery showing the Fault to be a giant V cleft, perhaps 8,000 ft in extent from mountain tops to bottom!

After two laborious days of sonaring, during which Bob Rines tried every means to check these persistent echo tracings, we put the equipment back on shore, and agreed that *Water Horse* had lived up to her famous reputation of being a 'lucky boat'.

The Americans flew west, and on 24 July I pulled her out for storage. Home again for two months, I struggled with a mountain of correspondence and family business, before travelling to Glasgow to attend a children's book show there.

After the show, I met Jim Buchanan, a scientist from Stirling University. As a marine biologist he had an interest in diving, and had recently formed his own film-making company, 'Undersea Vision (Scotland) Ltd'. We had met briefly the year before at Loch Ness when he was diving to investigate curious mound-like structures discovered near Aldourie Pier. Bob Rines had lent him the Edgerton strobe-camera with which to take underwater pictures of them.

Jim had invited me to crew on *Malaran* and journey by sea to Fort William, and so on to Loch Ness. *Malaran* was a 12-ton vessel in fibreglass with twin 50 h.p. diesels. I had always wanted to make this unique passage, which *Cizara* had navigated with the Smiths aboard in 1968 – and as Bob Rines expected to be back at Loch Ness for more sonar tests during the last week in September, Mr James

Ferrier, who owned and skippered the boat, had very kindly offered to put her at his disposal. *Malaran* had all 'mod cons' and a large wheelhouse with good visibility.

Mr Ferrier was a member of the Royal Glasgow Yacht Club, and we motored out towards it, eyeing the rough water in the Firth of Clyde. Once on board *Malaran*, we hung on while the mooring was slipped and the engines started to thrust her out into the channel. We departed in sheets of spray, waving goodbye to those on shore.

Three hours later, in Loch Fyne, it was pitch black, and we could only steer by the distant winking lights of buoys, checked off on the chart. It was a dangerous coastline, and I knew that if we struck we would never see the obstruction. But by 11 p.m. we had dropped the hook safely at Tarbert, a tiny pocket of a fishing port, and next morning early with ominous cherry-red painting the horizon, we forged on to the canal basin at Ardrishaig; where a 'puffer' unloaded coal, and the great circumnavigating yacht *Adventure* was preparing for sea. By mid afternoon we were through to Crinan.

Storm warnings were loud on the radio, and boats were coming in for shelter. We left and headed out into the Sound of Jura, then through the tidal rips of Scarba, past the legendary Straits of Corryvreckan, with its whirlpools, and out into the Firth of Lorne.

There was a big swell coming in from the Atlantic, and the skipper decided to alter course for shelter. With *Malaran* pointing her bows to the sky one moment and down into the depths the next, she slid and wallowed a way to safety – to the rock-enclosed cove of Puilladohrain, and here she lay for the next thirty-six hours, while the wind roared above us in gales of up to 'storm force 10'. The day was 21 September, 'Equinoctial Storm Day', as I had come to think of it – and we were lucky to be safe.

On 22 September the wind had moderated and we left for Oban, running with the great moving swells of water, and went ashore there. Time was pressing, and with some anxiety we put out across the Firth of Lorne. It was a difficult crossing in search of sheltered water, and so on up through the Corran Narrows with engines blaring at full throttle against an 8-knot tidal rip.

Arriving off Fort William, in Lochaber, as it was known in song, we dropped the hook at Camusnan-gal. It was too late to enter the sea lock at Corpach, and the canal through the Great Glen. The passage from Greenock, with all its unexpected difficulty, had taken 4 days and another day was to pass before we tied up above the locks at Fort Augustus. On 24 September we moved down through them and on to Loch Ness. It was cold and windy but we drifted *Malaran* all day, monster-hunting. Before we cast off next morning a man approached us and introduced himself as 'Commander Bellars'. He was monster-hunting too, having been witness to a good two-hump sighting, when touring the loch with his family in 1972. He had been reported in the local press at the time, and had given details to the LNI. As a recently-retired anti-submarine officer in the Royal Navy, Commander Bellars' account was all the more impressive – and he was promptly inducted as a member of the crew aboard *Malaran*, as she moved out quietly and headed for Urquhart Bay.

On the way up he recorded his experience on tape, from which it appeared that the two humps protruded about 4 ft above the water – looked something like 'upturned boats' and together measured some 40 ft from front to rear. There had been no boats in the vicinity at the time, and the humps disappeared while the Bellars family car was being driven along General Wade's road towards them, to get a better view.

Calling in at Urquhart Bay, we made contact with the Americans who had just come in by air, and on 26 September, after collecting batteries, transducers and equipment, Bob and Carol Rines came aboard, and the sonar test runs were made confirming the results obtained in July, which had so astounded the experts in America. The rock-walls beneath the bottom were again clearly defined, and no amount of double-echo checking could disprove them.

The explanation of how the signal and its echo could penetrate the silt to such a remarkable depth seemed to indicate that water must be saturating it together with, perhaps, a pulp of vegetable debris swept into the loch over the centuries. Together they might become a permeable medium for the sonar pulse. It was a nice theory, but no more than that. Much additional work would need to be done to classify these soundings, but as Mr Ferrier was concerned about the threat of weather on the homeward journey, and the pending closure of the Crinan canal for repairs, *Malaran* could stay no longer, so we went about, and thundered back to Fort Augustus.

Next morning Bill Bellars and I helped *Malaran* up through the locks before going ashore with our kit. We met and talked with the Americans again and with the help of Dick Raynor, old *Fussy Hen* the LNI workboat was pressed into service in Urquhart Bay. Bob Rines wanted to do some final checks with the sonar, and off Urquhart Castle we mapped the strange underwater mount, 400–500 ft in height, coming up from the bottom. Evidence of this had first appeared as a fixed echo in the Birmingham sonar tests of 1968, had been seen by *Pisces* in 1969, and had since been traced in improved form on the chart recorders used by Dr Rines. Now we could see it in every detail.

Later in the day we inspected *Hunter*, which Jim Ewing had towed up from the south for us to use in 1975. She was put in storage temporarily, but her use in conjunction with a boathouse would give the Academy a step-on, step-off impetus to their underwater work, which was badly needed. Waterborne experiments were very time-consuming.

On 30 September, our last watching day, I introduced Bill Bellars to some friends of mine, only to find that but 3 hours previously they had watched a huge hump-like object with a 'tail' floating motionless off the Horse Shoe scree – through × 10 binoculars. It was not a boat, and resembled 'a huge warty bladder'. After 20 minutes or so it just disappeared. They reckoned it to be about 50 ft in length.

This tremendous dimension, if it in fact related to the Monster, was in keeping with other such reports, raising again the question of species – could the Monster be a reptile, a mammal, a fish, a mollusc, an amphibian, a psychic phenomenon, or just plain spots before the eyes? No one could tell for sure, but in relation to the 'amphibian theory' which Commander Gould had plumped for in the early 1930s, it was interesting to read in Nicholas Witchell's excellent historical work *The Loch Ness Story* that Professor Roy Mackal of Chicago University regarded it as a possible first choice, apropos of 'some evolutionary derivative of a primitive aquatic amphibian of a species called the embolomer, found in the Carboniferous period about 270 million years ago'.

Of all the theories, the 'amphibian theory' was one of the most elegant, if not improbable – for they all appeared improbable – and when reading a beautifully illustrated old book recently, *The Outdoor World* published in 1905, I noted that in reference to 'The Great Warty Newt' it was stated that: 'This newt hibernates during the winter months, and for the whole of this time the lungs are inactive, the creature deriving the small air-supply necessary for its indolent existence through its skin.' Could such performance, I wondered, explain the long periods when the Monster appeared to be inactive? Amphibians were also noted for their metamorphosis of shape, and as Ivan Sanderson once pointed out in an article – in some cases for gigantism, when the latter stages of metamorphosis failed to develop.

However, from a practical standpoint, whatever Monsters exist in Loch Ness or Loch Morar today, the question of how they got there cannot be avoided, because the Great Glen cleft was filled with ice during the last Ice Age. After that, as far as we know, it became an arm of the sea when the ice melted; then as the land rose slowly, as it is doing today, the lochs were formed in it, of which Loch Ness is the largest. Thus, *ipso facto*, the Monsters must have come from the sea originally, and I do not know of any marine amphibian which even approached the scale reported for the Monsters. To some extent this applies to the Plesiosaurs, the largest of which with the longest neck only grew to about 40 ft in length, but they were totally adapted for life at sea, except for the females, which were thought to lay their eggs in estuaries. The Plesiosaurs had great diamond-shaped paddles too, and were very fast predators which ate fish – or so it is thought of the long-necked variety.

However, it is not the purpose of this book to speculate, and whether the Monsters turn out to be amphibians, or Plesiosaurs, or giant eels, or giant long-necked seals or even sea-slugs, which are of an unknown species, or an evolved species of some previously known animal – only time, and man, will determine.

At the present time it is still true to say that the main search effort is made by private individuals, and small voluntary scientific groups, who have to buy, or borrow, or make their own equipment and pay their own expenses, but this does not mean they are not effective. And if these 'amateur' investigators appear to be unimpressed by the performance of the Establishment in this connection, it is interesting to recall the words of an ex-Establishment scientist, an ichthyologist of standing who had the following to say in the columns of the *Observer*, on 28 May 1961:

> If I am correct in believing that Science has more to do with an attitude of mind than with a body of dogmas or even knowledge, then I will go further and say there is more hope for Science in the enthusiastic amateurism of the Dinsdales and their like than there is in the institutionalised professionalism, the petrified respectability, the abject deference to Authority, the unreasoning fear of Press ridicule, the tender regard for tenderer reputations, and the yearnings toward the nomination lists at Burlington House which have kept qualified zoologists well away from Loch Ness this last thirty years.

But times change, and in fairness it is true to say that in 1972 Dr Rines and I were treated with courtesy and understanding when visiting the Keeper and Deputy Keeper of Zoology at the British Natural History Museum, to show the first results of the underwater photography obtained in Urquhart Bay – and this was before the computer-enhancement breakthrough on the 'flipper' photograph. It is also true that the Smithsonian in America has been helpful in attempting to assess it, and that this Institute sponsored the Wolper/CBS documentary, 'MONSTERS, Mysteries or Myths?', put out across the USA on 25 November 1974, in which the Yeti, Big Foot, and Loch Ness Monster phenomena were considered critically – and the fieldwork of Peter Byrne, Dr Rines and his Academy, myself and others was presented before a vast audience. This film received the highest interest rating of any documentary in American television history.

Index